THE DEBT WALL

Own Your Money < Own Your Future

PRAMOD DASH

ISBN
Paperback 979-8-89744-266-9
Hardcase 979-8-89906-965-9

CONTENTS

Chapter 1

INTRODUCTION

Money shapes your choices. Choices shape your future. Simple, but easy to ignore.

Managing money can feel for young people — and especially new graduates — like an attempt to solve a puzzle with missing pieces. This chapter isn't going to be a textbook kind of explanation. In fact, it's the one that tells true stories — about people like you making choices, struggling, winning, and falling short.

You'll be tracking a guy who got the first job of his life and thought he had it all resolved — until he opened the credit card bill. A woman with student loans and an unexpected medical bill is weighing calling her parents for help. Housemates split rent but disagree on

The point here is not to warm them up to the terms of money. It's to show how all those terms look on a daily basis. A budget is more than just a spreadsheet. It's a tool for liberating yourself from financial constraints. Debt is not just a number — it's a weight that can stifle aspirations if ignored. And saving isn't simply a concept — it allows you to say yes to opportunities without anxiety.

This chapter also looks at broader forces, not just individual stories. What do you think about the way that social media causes people to go into debt? What Are the Family Dynamics That Fuel Financial Choices? Why are some people always struggling and others getting ahead?

This is not a guide to dos and don'ts. This is a chronicle of moments, lessons, and awakenings. Some will be familiar. Others might be surprising. But all of them will help you walk away with useful frameworks for thinking about money and alternatives to consider. Most importantly, they will provide you with the confidence to regain control over your financial life.

The abundance of data and advice can easily overwhelm our minds. However, distinct narratives effectively penetrate the clutter. They turn big ideas into something small and real. They show how someone else faces a problem that looks a lot like yours.

Think of a recent graduate buried in piles of student debt and trying to launch their career. They learned how to climb out of debt, save, and even start a business. Theirs isn't simply a story of numerical success — it's a story of determination. It's like a friend telling you what worked for her."

And stories hit emotions. Consider the pressure to overspend on items such as clothes, a high-end cell phone, and extravagant nights out. Another man wrestled with those limitations and emerged free on the other side. When you hear that, you start to second-guess how you spend. Are your habits enabling you to evolve or keeping you static?

Stories are not mere lessons to be learned. They also reflect larger trends, like how expensive city life squeezes young professionals. A new worker in a large metro might spend 50% of their earnings on rent and transportation. And theirs is not just a personal struggle — it's part of a bigger trend. It gives you a backdrop for your own troubles that almost always enable you to navigate and find a path forward.

In this chapter, you'll meet people making choices, wrestling, succeeding, and failing at times, too. This is not a list of dos and don'ts. This is a compilation of my real-life experiences, realizations, and valuable lessons. Some will feel familiar. Others might surprise you. But each will change the way you look at money — and make you better equipped to seize control of it.

Forget everything you thought you knew about debt. The rules are different now, and if you ignore them, you could end up in a debt treadmill. From credit cards to housing loans and personal finance schemes, the way Indians borrow and spend has changed to a substantial extent in a matter of years. However, it's important to note that lenders have a deeper understanding of this game than most borrowers.

THE RISE OF EMI CULTURE IN INDIA

While the EMI model has become a way of life in India, it is not an exception. Consider this:

India is the country with the highest EMI purchases. In India, EMI accounts for 70% of iPhone purchases.

Loans finance 80% of all cars on the road.

Long-term EMIs finance 60% of home purchases.

The financial safety net that they once relied on — borrowing only when absolutely necessary — had shifted into a lifestyle choice. EMI is not regarded as a last resort — it is now a default method for buying high-ticket items. Once famously cash-happy, the Indian middle class has developed a Western dependence on credit. But here's the difficulty: Most people have no grasp of the cost of this transition.

THE TRUE COST OF EMI PURCHASES

EMIs feel comfortable, even innocuous. After all, why spend ₹1,50,000 in one go when you can divide it into "easy" ₹7,000 per month payments for your iPhone? Yet, there is a hidden danger — taking multiple EMIs without realizing the long-term financial implications.

Take the case of Rahul, a 28-year-old IT professional in Bengaluru. He began with a MacBook EMI. Then came the iPhone upgrade. A few months later, he secured a car loan. By the time he turned 30, EMI had shackled half his salary, making disposable income a myth. He appeared to be living a luxurious lifestyle. But in fact, he was one surprise bill away from financial calamity.

EMI culture runs on one illusion: affordability. But affordability does not mean something is cheap; it just means you can distribute payments over time. The real question is, what's the full picture of how much money you're actually on the hook for? High interest rates, sneaky processing fees, and delinquent payment penalties—all of these add up and turn your "affordable payment" into far less of a bargain than purchasing it outright.

Chapter 2

WINNERS AND LOSERS IN INDIA'S NEW DEBT ECONOMY

Debt always divides people into two groups: those in control and those ensnared by it. The financially savvy obtain loans strategically — to invest in appreciating assets such as homes or businesses. However, those without sight will find themselves ensnared in a cycle, working solely to meet their monthly bills.

Let us examine some real-life examples.

Neha's Home Loan Nightmare

Neha, a Pune-based schoolteacher, took a home loan in 2018 when the interest rates were low. She also budgeted her finances carefully, making sure that her EMI did not go beyond 30% of her monthly salary. But post the repo rate hikes in 2022 her EMI increased by 40% of her salary a month. She had not factored in the rising interest rates, and now she's struggling to meet payments — which has made her cut back on essentials to be in the green.

ARVIND'S CREDIT CARD TRAP

Arvind, a marketing executive in Delhi, used a credit card to finance a family vacation and thought he would be able to pay it off in a few months. But he made only the minimum payment each month. What he didn't know was that his outstanding debt was earning 36% interest per year. When he added up his receipts, he discovered he had spent almost twice what he would have paid if he had done the calculations beforehand. A modest vacation (turned into) didn't just become a 2-year financial burden instead.

HOW TO BE DEBT-FREE AND OUT OF THE EMI TRAP

To stay aloft in India's changing credit economy, you must have a strategy. Here's how you can get to take control:

1. ***Understand the True Cost of Debt***

    Always calculate how much you'll pay overall, over the length of the loan.

    Check the fine print — hidden fees and penalties can increase your cost.

    An EMI may appear affordable, but that doesn't mean it's financially prudent.

2. ***Prioritize High-Interest Debt***

    You should attack credit card balances and personal loans first — they bear the highest interest rates.

    Employ the avalanche method: Focus on your highest-interest debt while paying the minimum on any others.

3. ***Negotiate Everything***

    Banks don't advertise this, but you can negotiate interest rates, particularly if you have a strong credit score.

    Ask for waivers on late fees and for flexible repayment terms.

4. ***Build a Financial Cushion***

    Keep an emergency fund on hand to prevent unexpected debt.

    Try to set aside at least six months of expenses.

5. ***Use Credit to Your Advantage***

    Use credit cards wisely to develop a strong credit score — never carry one from month to month.

    Consider government-backed loan programs for lower rates.

What you can do: Refinance loans or transfer balances to ease your repayment load.

DEBT IS A TOOL, NOT A TRAP

Debt isn't bad. How you use it will chart your financial fate. The rich use debt to acquire assets — buying real estate, investing in businesses. The financially illiterate take on debt for liabilities: financing for cars, gizmos, and vacations.

Which side do you want to be?

The simple truth is: If you fail to manage your debt, it will ultimately control you. Only those who take the time to learn will last as the financial world shifts.

So, consider this — are you using debt to build wealth, or is debt using you?

EMI trap: Time to break free from its clutches; the choice is yours.

MONEY AND SOCIAL PRESSURES

Money influences the world in more ways than bank accounts. It is linked to culture, family, and even geography.

Property and gold mean financial success in India, and families are proud of these investments. But are they the best choice for those starting out? Maybe. Maybe not. The best approach is to do what you want, not what tradition you want to follow.

Social media makes it worse. Scroll through Instagram. Just scroll through influencers in exotic locations, wearing designer clothing and the latest tech. If you're not privy to what's going on, you feel that you're missing out. That pressure can drive you into debt. But whose approval are you pursuing? Strangers online? Or your own goals?

City life drains money fast. Rent eats up paychecks. Food costs more. So does getting around. You may constantly feel behind schedule. However, acknowledging these realities can significantly impact your situation. Maybe you will discover a less expensive locale. Perhaps you stopped ordering things that you didn't really need. Small shifts add up.

The trick is to identify the pressures based on what they are. The next step is to take control of your own priorities.

LIVING ON BORROWED MONEY: THE NEW NORMAL

And you think there are so many, many paths to ruin — use of illicit drugs. But they do. Or rather, they appear to. For behind the glossy façade of aspirational living is a creaking reliance on Equated Monthly Instalments (EMIs) — a financial phenomenon that is reconfiguring how Indians spend, save, and even feel about money.

The numbers paint the picture:

In India, EMI accounts for 70% of iPhone purchases.

Since EMIs finance 80% of the vehicles on the road, this term is appropriate and defined in the context of automobiles.

60% of homes are purchased with home loans, paid back over decades.

These figures reveal a profound shift in financial life, where the ability to service debt, rather than wealth, determines ownership.

But is this sustainable? Or are we building a future in which the average Indian is locked in a cycle of bottomless repayments?

FROM FRUGALITY TO EMI DEPENDENCY

Only a generation ago, taking out loans for the sake of nonessential purchases seemed unthinkable. Parents saved for years to buy a car. A home was a once-in-a-lifetime purchase, something to consider only when finances were solid. Credit cards were for emergencies, not impulse purchases.

That way of thinking has shifted today. No need to wait; you can have it today! Now, banks, fintech companies, and consumer brands have made borrowing easier than ever. Zeroth down payment schemes, instant approvals, and BNPL (buy now, pay later) models have made debt normal and seem like a more prudent way to live with money than financial risk.

The shift was accounted for by:

Aggressive marketing by banks and Non-Banking Financial Company (NBFCs) – Banks and NBFCs now actively encourage consumers to apply for loans at every opportunity. Pre-approved credit limits and 'easy finance' schemes make borrowing feel too easy.

Aspirational consumerism — Owning the latest iPhone, driving a luxury SUV, or living in a premium apartment isn't just about convenience, it's about social status.

Inflation and stagnant incomes – When salaries do not keep pace with the cost of living, EMIs are the only way to buy things that were once attainable with savings.

The True Cost of Easy Credit

EMIs appear to be a mutually beneficial arrangement. Now you get what you want and pay the price, small and manageable, over time. But underneath it, there's a dirty secret — a lifetime of payments that can easily get out of hand.

Here's how it plays out:

An EMI iPhone: If you take a ₹1,00,000 iPhone on a 12-month EMI with 14% interest, the final cost of that phone will be ₹1,07,800.

A car loan: A ₹10 lakh car on a 5-year EMI with 10% interest ends up being at₹12.7 lakh.

Home loan: ₹50 lakh home loan — 8% for 20 years? The total you pay is almost ₹1 crore.

Borrowing begs more borrowing to pay off the old debt, delaying pay-off longer. And unlike the U.S. or Europe, where lower interest rates make borrowing a little less painful, India's high interest rates guarantee that most people will end up paying much more than they originally borrowed.

THE MIDDLE-CLASS DEBT TRAP

EMIs give the impression of prosperity for the Indian middle class. You're earning ₹80,000 a month, but a ₹40,000 home loan, ₹15,000 car EMI, ₹5,000 phone EMI, and miscellaneous credit card dues leave you with dirt—no savings. One job loss, a medical crisis, or a recession can cause the entire financial situation to collapse.

It's not uncommon for lenders to discuss EMIs. The pitch is always about affordability—"Just ₹3,999 per month and this gadget can be yours!" But they don't stress how these "small" payments add up, ensnaring people in long-term financial traps that make it impossible to create wealth.

GETTING UNSTUCK: GOOD DEBT VS. BAD DEBT

EMIs aren't inherently bad. Appropriately applied, they can be a beneficial resource to stabilize cash flow and purchase necessary equipment. The trick is to distinguish between good debt and bad debt:

Good Debt: Debt taken on for assets that 1) increase in value or 2) produce income (college education, mortgage on first home, business investment)

Negative Debt: EMIs for luxury purchases, vacations, and high-interest rate credit card debt or lifestyle costs.

STEPS TO AVOID THE EMI TRAP

Follow the 30% Rule – Don't let your overall EMI load cross 30% of your monthly income.

Don't Fall for No-Down Payment Offers — If You Can't Afford a Down Payment, You Probably Can't Afford the Product

Pay Off Loans Early — No matter what, if you can pay off loans early, do it, because it saves you interest.

Control High-Interest EMIs – There are credit card EMIs that charge interest rates from 18-24%. Use these only when required.

Save First, Borrow Later – Instead of getting an EMI for the next gadget or vacation, consider a reverse EMI—saving a monthly amount and buying with it.

CONCLUSION: WE NEED A SHIFT IN CULTURE

India is facing a pivotal moment. Although the EMI culture has made it easier for people to fulfill their dreams, it does so at the cost of long-term financial health. A country that once prided itself on living within its means has slowly become more reliant on credit. If things go on like this, the future is a debt crisis where millions struggle to get the payments done.

You cover a lot of ground here, and the objective of this book is not to preach against borrowing but rather to get into the habit of responsible borrowing. Before every EMI decision, ask yourself—is this a need, or am I purchasing a lifestyle that I cannot really afford?

In a society where everything is available on an installment plan, real financial autonomy is measured in what you don't owe as much as in what you own.

SETTING THE STAGE FOR SUCCESS

It is easier to budget good money when you have goals. Awareness of what prompts your factors keeps you focused.

Chunk it into manageable parts — saving, spending, handling debt. It's kind of like making a playlist. Some of them survived today. Some set you up for what happens next.

Maybe you're putting away money for a trip. Or build an emergency fund. It's more than just money. It's confidence that you can handle life's curveballs. Small wins matter. Avoiding impulsive purchases is crucial. Reaching a savings goal is crucial. Each step builds momentum.

There are tools to help. Budgeting apps track where your cash is going. They show where you might be open to compromise. Tiny tweaks add up. What was once daunting is now a series of simple pulls.

CLOSING THOUGHTS

This chapter won't teach you how to budget or save. It's about proving financial independence is 100% possible and possible regardless of where you start from.

They will share personal stories, practical advice, and real challenges that are relevant to young people today. Also, you'll see how they persevere. The goal? The goal is to equip them with tools that will enable them to make better choices.

You're not in this alone. They've navigated debt, resisted social pressures, and figured out how to make life work in expensive cities. Their stories demonstrate how it is possible. With a method that works for you, you can own your money and live however you want.

THE FINANCIAL EVOLUTION IN INDIA

India's relationship with money and borrowing has undergone a seismic shift over the last several years. People have stopped asking friends and family to lend a hand. Instead, they will turn to banks and financial institutions. This shift isn't only about using new tools — it highlights profound changes in mindsets about how people deploy money and chase their dreams.

Such shifts have loomed largest among young professionals, college students and recent graduates. Many are reassessing financial planning, debt management and personal savings. Rapid urbanization and a growing middle class have made it easier to get loans for housing, emergencies and even for lifestyle upgrades.

Government policy, favorable economic conditions, and financial literacy programs also help. Determine how consumers borrow and use credit. The attitudes toward loans have changed over the years. Borrowing now isn't the terrifying last resort; it's the manageable tool that, done well, can improve quality of life.

High interest rates and new market trends spurred public sentiment in the other direction. The proliferation of credit cards, buy-now-pay-later schemes, and easy loan access has normalized debt. But where there's convenience, there's a bit of caution. Understanding these trends can help inform young people about financial decision-making.

This chapter unpicks these changes. It shows how wealth has evolved in the country and how people can take control of their own fate. But it isn't just borrowing, it's making money work for you.

INCREASE IN HOME AND PERSONAL LOANS

India's borrowing patterns have changed radically in the past few decades. What began as just covering basic needs — and largely relying on informal loans from family or friends — has evolved into an expansive, formalized system of credit. In those days, the majority of bank loans were for agriculture or business. However, banks have devised various personal and home loan schemes over the years, revolutionizing borrowing perceptions. This change is more than simply an increase in the number of products; it is also a sign of broader economic changes and growing attitudes about the role of credit in everyday life.

The growing middle class has driven this transition. And as cities sprawl and incomes increase, people are not simply dreaming bigger; they are pursuing those big dreams. Families have moved into urban space; home loans have exploded and became a kind of front-end-target financing for fulfilling that demand." The younger generation, by contrast, is reimagining credit. They view loans not as debts but as levers — devices used to purchase better homes, better cars, better education, or even travel. This newfound openness to borrowing signals a dramatic cultural shift, as credit now serves as a tool for creating opportunities rather than a last resort for emergency situations.

The rapid expansion of the middle class closely correlates with the rising demand for loans. The march of urbanization and economic growth has greatly expanded the number of Indians with spending power, and their aspirations for lifestyle upgrades are unsurprising — homes, cars, education, and travel. As cities expand at an accelerated pace, urban areas are increasingly home to families — a key driver of the demand for housing finance. And there has been a cultural shift among a younger generation — one that is willing to take on debt to realize personal and professional goals. This demographic is also particularly hungry to upgrade their lifestyles through credit, which has transformed into less weight and more of a path to opportunity.

Recent government interventions have had an amazing impact on borrowers' way of looking at loans, washing completely in their own way the convenience and desirability of such facilities. And new programs have helped keep borrowing much easier — and more alluring — than in the past. To increase engagement, use a more colorful word: But affordable interest rates for housing loans and simple mortgage processes are making it a reality for millions of people. Such efforts are about more than trimming costs; they have served to mitigate a sense of existential confusion and anxiety that often stalks financial systems.

The lower rates, along with other economic changes, have played a role in the increasing use of loans. This is why several Indians prefer purchase via loan; many loan products are also much cheaper as that is the best way to buy exorbitant assets or achieve certain investment targets. With lower rates, it's also cheaper to meet monthly obligations on mortgages and personal loans, enabling families to balance their finances without straining their budgets.

That climate, in turn, also draws more people to the idea of borrowing as an efficient way to create needs or goals. Simply put, the job has been made easy with the number of public awareness programs that are directly reaching people to educate them on financial literacy. They have helped everyday people learn how to better manage debt so that they feel more comfortable and confident making informed decisions about borrowing.

THE FALL OF MOM-AND-POP SHOPS

Mom-and-Pop stores were community glue, and for decades, family-owned businesses were the binders. One example is a corner dinner. The establishment also houses a small hardware store.

The morning bakery served fresh bread. These weren't just shopping havens. They served as gathering places for people. You knew the owner. You swapped stories. Your money stayed local. It meant something.

Now? Almost gone. They have been devoured by chains. Fast food. Big-box stores. The exchanges are impersonal and anonymous, taking place in sterile spaces. No names. No familiarity. This is just another card swipe.

It's not just about money. Something deeper got lost. A sense of place. A rhythm. A connection.

THE CORNER CAFÉ: A FAMILIAR STORY

Take Sharma Ji's Dhaba. It was a neighborhood favorite for over 50 years. The Sharma family operated it, selling hot parathas, chai, and homestyle dishes. They didn't come only for food. They would arrive to engage in conversation, exchange local rumors, and relish the positive outlook.

And then it came to a big fast-food chain. They launched ₹99 meal combos — it cost Sharma Ji more than that to procure fresh ingredients. Flashy billboards, Internet ads, and discount coupons flooded the area.

Sharma Ji's Dhaba shut down a year later. The family resold the space and went back to their village.

It was more than the loss of a dhaba for the locals. It was the loss of a gathering spot — somewhere people mingled, bonded, and felt at home.

Why Small Businesses Struggle

The numbers explain why so many kirana stores and small businesses barely survive:

Rising Costs

Shop rent: ₹25,000/month

Three workers' salaries: ₹30,000/month

Rent (office): ₹10,000/month Electricity, water, and supplies: ₹12,000/month

Monthly expenses per month: ₹67,000/month

Such a shop necessitates consistent profits to weather economic fluctuations. But major supermarket chains and online platforms purchase in bulk, offer steep discounts, and draw consumers in with flashy promotions. Small businesses, compelled to meet the prices, see their margins deteriorate. The fight isn't fair. Many go under before they have a chance to bounce back.

FALLING REVENUE

Ravi's kirana shop was doing well before the supermarket came. Sales figures ranged around ₹50,000 a day. It wasn't lavish, but it kept the shop afloat, paid bills, and provided for his family.

And then the big retail chain came along. Prices were lower. Discounts never stopped. Everything was conveniently located under one roof. Customers drifted away.

Ravi was down to ₹20,000 a day in sales. A ₹30,000 monthly shortfall.

He tried to hold on. He sought financial assistance from his friends. He then obtained the loan from a local moneylender. Loan repayments stacked up. Late fees followed. The store that once provided stability was now sinking him into debt.

MARKET SHARE SHIFT

Some 92% of India's retail market in 1990 was made up of small shops and street-based vendors.

By 2025, that proportion had dropped to 55%.

Who took their place? Supermarkets. E-commerce giants. These slick, convenient, heavily bankrolled behemoths purported to save you money but ultimately crushed small store owners in the process.

THE RIPPLE EFFECT:

When a small business closes, it affects more than the owners.

JOB LOSS

Small businesses account for a large share of the workforce in India. When they close, livelihoods vanish.

At Gupta Ji's Tea Stall, workers who once had steady income now work in less secure jobs at large café chains. Some took pay cuts. Others face erratic schedules. The coziness of working for a familiar, local employer is vanishing — replaced by demanding hours and corporate policies that don't flex.

ECONOMIC DRAIN

Money stays in the community with local businesses. Studies show:

Spending 67 paisa of rupees in a local shop keeps money in the local economy.

Just 43 paisa per rupee stays in the community at big retail chains.

The closure of small shops has ripple effects beyond lost businesses. That translates to less money for local schools, roads, and public services. The neighborhood isn't just losing a shop — it's losing financial backing that keeps it afloat.

LOSS OF CHARACTER

All these locations have the same plants. Bazaars turn into malls. Chai stalls disappear. Local flavors fade.

When every street has the same supermarket, the same fast-food chain, and the same clothing store, what's there to call unique? Neighborhoods become unrecognizable."

If somewhere can only claim, "It looks like every other city," what's to be so proud about?

REVISITING MYSORE CAFE'S DEFEAT

A deep dive into **Sharma Ji's Dhaba** defeat

Here's what happened with Sharma Tiffin Center:

Town population: 10,000

Typical family expenditure on eating out: ₹3,000/year

Before the chain restaurants came:

70% of that spending was on local eateries, or ₹2,100/year per household.

After local restaurants closed:

Expenditure moved to larger chains.

Local economy total loss: ₹86 lakh per year.

COMPUTATION: LET US DISSECT:

Population = 10 000

Average Household Size = 5

Average Restaurant Expenditure per Family (annually) = ₹3,000

Percentage of Spending That Went to Local Businesses Before Closures: 70% (or 0.70)

After local restaurants shut down:

- Spending shifted to big chains.
- Total local economic loss: ₹42 lakh per year.
- Money flowing out to corporate giants: ₹18 lakh per year.

This cycle saps local wealth and undermines small businesses and community growth year after year.

WHY IT MATTERS

Losing Kirana stores, family-run cafés, and street vendors isn't just about money. It's about losing a way of life.

Local businesses build relationships. The shopkeeper knows your name. The chaiwala remembers how you like your tea. The dosa stall owner asks about your family.

Big chains? They run fast. Standardization. Profit margins. The machine in question is a unique type.

When **Sharma Ji's Dhaba** shut down, the city didn't just lose a restaurant. It lost its meeting place. There were no more familiar voices. There were no warm welcomes. Just another vacant spot, waiting to be replaced by a logo instead of a legacy.

INDIA'S CHANGING CONSUMER SPENDING TRENDS: FROM SAVING TO EMIS

A Look at Two Eras

In the 1990s, it was rare to borrow. People took out loans only for big-ticket items — a wedding, a medical catastrophe, or a first house. Everything else? I saved for it, planned for it, and waited for it.

My father rides his bike to work every day. His old cycle was dependable and straightforward. A scooter? That was an expensive treat, no small matter, requiring years of saving. That wasn't just about convenience; it was a point of pride.

Fast forward to today. The streets reveal another story. Scooters outnumber cycles. People use cars more often than scooters. People use cars more often than scooters.

This is not just a shift in what people possess. It's a shift in how they own. Loans make it all feel attainable. You can afford a car now, rather than waiting five years to buy one. A house should be purchased at the age of thirty, not fifty.

But there's a cost. Easy loans come with a lengthy commitment. You make the payments in installments. Year after year, it passes. Before most of them realize it, they find themselves trapped — living on borrowed money and using future income to cover the costs of their past decisions.

TOXIC DEBT — THE LOAN CULTURE, A DOUBLE-EDGED SWORD

The balance in India's relationship with money has had a flip. Loans fuel everything now.

When my father was young, borrowing meant something. It took effort. The process involved persuading the bank to grant your request. You must demonstrate your need for money. Letting them borrow wasn't simply a transaction but a duty.

Now? Just a few taps on the phone will do the trick. Instant approvals. There are also pre-approved credit lines available. There are also offers that require no down payment. Banks, apps, and credit card companies pitch loans as festival discounts.

Buy now, pay later. Sounds easy. Feels harmless. But the payments do not just disappear. They piled up. The accumulation continues month after month. The cycle continues year after year. Debt gradually engulfs you, trapping you in its grasp.

SCENARIO 1: YOUR TWO-WHEELER FANTASY

The balance in India's relationship with money has reversed. Loans fuel everything now.

When my father was a young man, borrowing meant something. It took effort. The process involved persuading the bank to grant your request. You must demonstrate your need for money. You had to justify every rupee. Lending them wasn't a transaction; it was a responsibility.

Now? Just a few taps on the phone will do the trick. There are also pre-approved credit lines available. There are also offers that require no down payment. Instant approvals. Banks, apps, and credit card companies market loans as a festival discount.

EDUCATION: AT ONE TIME AFFORDABLE, NOW A DEBT TRAP

In the 1990s, the cost of college was affordable. There were fewer government institutions and fewer fees. Private colleges were rare. We have devised educational plans that haven't completely depleted the budget.

My dad graduated debt-free. He didn't need to weigh tuition against survival. Even a degree came without a price tag of stress.

Today? Different world. Education is a business. The private ones also demand payment in lakhs. Feel the climb every year. Now middle-tier families cannot keep up.

You can't afford to choose student loans. They're a necessity. Forget the years of EMIs along with a degree. Young college graduates enter their careers already in debt. They find themselves in debt even before they receive their first paycheck.

Higher education provides opportunities. But before that, it ensnares students in repayments.

SCENARIO 2: TAKING OUT LOANS TO FULFILL MBA DREAMS

Priya hails from a middle-class family in Chennai. Her dream? A decent private college MBA. The cost? ₹12 lakh.

There was no way to pay upfront. Her parents didn't have the means for it. There was no way forward except for a loan."

She took it. Finished her degree. Got a decent job.

Freedom didn't come with that job offer, however. Her salary wasn't hers for the next five years. Monthly EMIs drained out a large portion of her salary

Buying a house? Delayed.

Saving for retirement? Pushed back.

Building wealth? Developing wealth is not even a thought.

The degree provided opportunities. But first, it tethered her to repayment.

HOUSING: FROM SEMANTICS TO MORTGAGES

Owning a house was once a dream of a lifetime.

My father saved for years. One by one, he laid the bricks in our home. No loans. No EMIs. This requires patience, hard work, and discipline. It had taken him ten years, but once completed, it was entirely his.

Today, the banks make homeownership easier — to a point. Loans are everywhere. Low-interest rates. The loan comes with extended repayment periods. You can purchase a home today and make payments over the next 25 years.

It sounds like freedom. But is it?

EMIs eat into salaries. This pushes back financial goals. The bank maintains ownership of the house until the final payment clears. One missed EMI? Late fees. Higher interest. There is a pressing need to act quickly.

Convenience has a price. And it's paid for in decades.

SCENARIO 3: THE DREAM HOME

Amit and Neha – a young couple based in Pune—recently bought their dream 2BHK. The price? ₹75 lakh. The commitment? A 20-year home loan.

The excitement was real. Becoming a homeowner seemed like a significant milestone in life. It served as a symbol of stability.

But then the hidden costs came in. Maintenance. Property tax. Society fees. Repairs. None of it was in their initial playbook.

Half of the joint paycheck disappeared every month in EMIs and maintenance. Their budget shrank. There was no space left for vacations. There was no room for major investments. Even emergencies seemed like a financial risk.

The house was theirs. But their financial freedom? Disappeared for the next two decades.

BUY NOW AFFILIATIONS AND THE CULTURE OF IMMEDIATE GRATIFICATION

Consumer spending has changed with easy loans. No-cost EMIs. Instant approvals. Buy now, pay later.

This is well known to e-commerce platforms. They push it hard. Flash sales. Limited time offers. Deals that vanish within minutes. The pressure is real. Click. Swipe. Own.

A ₹1 lakh phone? No problem. Spend ₹4,000 a month for two years. A high-end laptop? Just another EMI.

It feels effortless. But those little payments add up. Before they can say "poly" they're handling several loans at a time. Salaries shrink under EMIs. Savings? Forgotten.

Spending time is easy. Paying it back? That's the real price.

SCENARIO 4: THE LATEST IPHONE

Arjun, 22, a student in college, did not need a new phone. His old one worked just fine.

Well But then the new iPhone came out, and the ads stayed on the air. No-cost EMI. Just ₹5,000 a month. It felt easy. Manage to sell for less than the value of an item.

Until reality hit.

₹5,000 wasn't small anymore. It meant skipping meals. Book-for-borrow instead of book-for-buying Not going out with friends.

The phone was sleek. The payments weren't. Luxury became a burden.

IMPACT OF SOCIAL MEDIA ON SPENDING

India's social media market is during a boom. As influencers, ads and viral trends shape our vistas; every swipe affects how we spend. This is a fact that young adults, students, and graduates should be aware of. They peddle ideas and wishes, as well as ways of life. If you don't exercise caution, they may manipulate you into making unnecessary purchases.

Trends can manifest as a fashion label, a device, or a skincare regime. The deluge of influences has turned them into a necessity. They're not. Every post promotes the same products. The more you hear, the more it seems like a must-have. All it takes is the first game to realize you want something you didn't even want a week ago.

Social media relies heavily on comparisons. Someone's vacation. They are enjoying their new car. They have acquired the newest model of phone.

Scrolling turns into a race of how far behind you can stay. The urge to spend follows. Sometimes, it even means taking out loans to build a brand. At that point, the situation becomes more challenging.

Algorithms watch everything. They monitor every like and click. They analyze what hinders your progress and then flood your feed with offers. Ads are not ads anymore. They're woven in, designed to feel organic. And before you know it, you've rationalized another purchase.

So how do you push back? Awareness. Recognize when you're under influence. Do you actually want — need — it, or did it wind up in front of you so frequently?

Set clear financial goals. A budget helps. When you know what matters to you, you're less susceptible to impulse purchases.

Wait before buying. Do you see something on social media? Pause. Give it a few days. If the need lessens, then you know it was not one.

Do some reading about the basics of personal finance. Budgeting. Credit. Saving.

The more knowledge you possess, the less susceptible you are to manipulation. Raising awareness can also work against you in this situation. Ironically, social media can help, but not in the way you might think. Follow financial educators rather than product peddlers.

And finally, cut the fluff from your feed. Mute the noise. Unfollow spending triggers. You need to be in touch with ideas and news. For in the power of money, financial freedom outranks any trend.

GOVERNMENT'S ROLE IN SHAPING FINANCIAL BEHAVIOR

These government schemes are changing Indians' perceptions of loans.

Homeownership, long a distant dream for many, is now within reach. Cost reduction through schemes like Pradhan Mantri Awas Yojana makes banks more amenable to lending. Lower interest rates. Easier approvals. The government is providing real assistance to first-time buyers.

It's changing mindsets too. Young professionals, recent college grads — people who wouldn't have considered the idea before — say they can buy a home now; buying a home is within reach. It's a goal, not a gambling.

Real estate Making money in real estate is no longer just for the wealthy. These programs not only stimulate the housing market, but they also fundamentally transform people's attitudes towards borrowing.

Part of the push comes from financial literacy. The government, banks, private institutions, and everyone else contribute to this effort. Free workshops. Online courses. These courses offer straightforward and useful guidance. That's a good loan? What's the bad one? How do interest rates work? Why is credit score important?

Such information is very valuable for students and young employees. Many enter the labor market in debt — education debt, startup loans, family obligations. Understanding responsible borrowing can significantly impact one's financial situation. It's the gap between wise decisions and financial disaster.

Other loans: Personal loans are also more accessible. Mudra Yojana, for instance, provides unsecured loans to small enterprises. Tailors. Shopkeepers. Street vendors.

Those who once dreamed of living in a capital city are no longer there.

No middlemen. There are no unachievable circumstances. There are no conditions that are impossible to achieve. All you need is a fair shot at growth.

Loans for education behave similarly. More students can obtain degrees without bankrupting their families. Repayment plans are clearer. More options, less stress. A huge shift, financially — borrowing no longer eternally burdensome.

Then there's regulation. Consumer statutes don't allow banks to be evasive. There are no hidden clauses. There are no unexpected penalties. That way, borrowers understand exactly what they're getting into. That transparency matters. It gets ahead of unsafe lending practices before they get into personal crises.

The second layer of protection is the Insolvency and Bankruptcy Code. "If someone can't truly pay there's a process for that." Structured. Legal. There are no shady tactics involved. Lenders and borrowers both know the rules, and that lends confidence to the system.

Add all that together, and the impact is unmistakable. Indians are devising ideas that feminize financial independence. Loans are vectors now, not shackles. It's planned borrowing, not desperate borrowing.

For young adults, this is a pivotal moment. A generation raised to fear debt is learning how to use it. That switch — from avoiding to controlling — is what financial independence actually is.

LOVE-HATE RELATIONSHIP WITH DEBT

Amit, like many Indians, has a complicated history with debt. There are too many zeros in a 20-something living in Mumbai, Amit gleefully spent more than Amit could afford, borrowed to make up the difference until Amit maxed out Amit's credit cards. Amit was living (leading) beyond his means, putting himself in a debt hole with no true experience about how difficult it would be to climb out.

Credit was freely available, and the rush of enjoying a lifestyle Amit couldn't really afford was nice — until the bills started arriving.

Amit didn't do it alone on Amit's own. Eventually Amit married Amit's future wife, who pulled me out of Amit's financial mess with her savings after we got married. While this may not be an ideal start to a marriage, it is a common practice in many Indian households where families share the financial burden. Debt was another key deterministic factor in growing our wealth in the future. When Amit's wife and Amit purchased our first house in Pune in the mid-2000s, we availed ourselves of the largest home loan we could get. And it was an interest-only loan, too. We had no plans to pay off the principal, and we never did.

According to real estate listings, the house's value has more than doubled since we purchased it, and we have used the money we saved by not making any principal payments—roughly INR 7,00,000 to date—for house renovations. We renovated a modular kitchen and fully furnished an extra room. Hence, without that savings buffer, we may not have felt comfortable maxing out our PPF, SIPs, and contributing to our kids education fund.

I am not exactly sure what made Amit think that taking out such a huge loan was okay. Some people at the time told me it was too risky. But Amit knows that some of Amit's courage at least came from financial conversations with Amit's mentor, Rajesh Mehta, an investment adviser who had always pushed for calculated risks. We met in college, became friends, and have kept in touch ever since. Amit has been a financial journalist for much of his career and has met countless advisors, but Rajesh's insights always stood out. Rajesh approached finance with a unique and straightforward perspective, recognizing that debt, when used appropriately, can be a valuable tool, akin to a hammer or a nail. However, a hammer is not inherently useful unless it serves a specific purpose.

Almost all personal finance books available in India today are limited to behavioral psychology. They are full of hacks that feel good without actually advancing your financial position. For instance, some books advocate the payoff of your lowest-balance credit card before tackling the one that incurs the highest interest in order to feel a psychological victory. This may feel good in the short run, but ultimately, it will cost you in the long run.

Rajesh frequently questioned conventional wisdom. One of his most powerful arguments was that debt-free is not synonymous with wealth. Debt, if used right, he wrote, can be a ladder rather than a ball chain toward financial development.

Amit disagrees with Rajesh on one point, which is to do with Indian stock market valuations. He sees Indian markets as overpriced; long-term growth is likely underwhelming. However, I remain optimistic. Amit: Due to the expanding middle class, rapid digital adoption, and the strong fundamentals of the economy, we believe the markets will continue to provide substantial growth opportunities. But Rajesh and Amit disagree on one fundamental truth — "No one can predict the future with certainty". Even if interest rates remain lower for longer than the consensus really expects, and stock market returns beat expectations, now is the best time ever to adhere to solid principles of personal finance.

These insights are not just theory. They are designed to help you go from borrower to investor and make you financially independent. Announce the approach I've sketched here, not as an instant to-do list, but as a long-term game plan. I, like Amit, have also been through the whole debt-recovery-wealth-building cycle and can assure you that you can change your financial destiny by just having the right knowledge and taking calculated risks.

This chapter isn't just the story of Amit. It's a tale familiar to millions of Indians with the deceptive complexities of personal finance in an aspirational world. If you find yourself in debt today, take comfort in knowing that it's not the end of your journey. With discipline, the right strategies, and a long-term outlook, you can transform debt from a barrier into an opportunity.

ECONOMIC DRIVERS AND CONSUMER LENDING TRENDS

You may have observed as much in India. Borrowing is different now. More loans. More first-time buyers. Younger investors are making riskier financial moves.

Why? A few things line up. Cheap credit. The economy is robust.

Property prices are on the rise. People are moving to cities. All that helps push borrowing into the mainstream.

THE INTEREST RATE EFFECT

Low rates change everything. And banks make loans at rates that appear not to be a trap. A home loan? A business loan? Even personal loans? They're all more enticing when interest isn't suffocating.

When it comes to younger professionals, it's flexibility. Borrowing money doesn't have to wreck your budget. Lower monthly payments free up money for other things — education, investments, not to mention day-to-day expenses. Debt becomes manageable. It complements their lives instead of controlling them.

OPTIMISM DRIVES RISK

Confidence is high in a solid economy. More jobs. Better wages. There has been growth in various industries. If people think their financial future is rosy, they are more willing to borrow.

Students view degrees as an investment. Young employees borrow money to start businesses. Families bet their futures on homeownership. And the logic is basic — borrow now, pay back later, when salaries rise.

Of course, that's a gamble. But it's a risk that many are keen to take.

Property prices aren't waiting for anyone. Cities are expanding fast. Demand is relentless. The cost of living in large cities is getting more and more expensive.

For a lot of people, renting is a waste of money. So, owning a home seems like the more sensible choice. But saving up? Nearly impossible. That's where loans step in. The structured repayment plan makes homeownership feel within reach, even amid soaring prices.

MIGRATION ADDS PRESSURE

Millions migrate from rural villages to urban cities every year. They come for jobs, education, and a better life. However, cities lack the necessary infrastructure to manage such extreme conditions. Housing shortages. High rent. Packed hostels.

Loans give them an option. They can own it instead of paying rent indefinitely. Even new graduates consider home loans earlier than ever. It's not just about a roof over their heads — it's about their financial security.

LOANS AS A CULTURAL SHIFT

Not everyone understood debt this way. Parents warned against it. Borrowing meant struggle. But that mindset is changing.

Family support helps. Parents co-sign. Family members contribute. Younger generations see loans as a tool, not a burden. This doesn't need to be the same desperation to borrow anymore — it's about opportunity.

THE BIGGER PICTURE

Everything connects. There are low interest rates available. Migration. Rising wages. Real estate prices are on the rise. The three collectively shape how Indians borrow.

The takeaway for millennials is straightforward. Loans aren't the villains — but irresponsible borrowing is. Knowing why people borrow means knowing when it makes sense for you.

Debt should ultimately serve you, not the other way around.

THERE IS NO HERO IN THE DEBT CULTURE

This chapter examined how borrowing is redefining financial behaviors in India. Loans — once an occasional human necessity — became a regular activity. Home loans. Personal loans. Easy credit. More people can access them. More people rely on them.

A growing middle class stimulates demand. Bigger incomes. Bigger dreams. Families are relocating to urban areas. Government policies and banks are relaxing restrictions on borrowing. The cumulative effect is significant.

This phenomenon is not a huge deal for young adults. Loans are tempting. Interest rates are low. EMI plans seem manageable. But readily available money isn't free.

A single incorrect decision today can compound into years of financial hardship. The door's depth can open — as well as shut.

THE COST OF OVER-RELIANCE

One generation, which has borrowed too easily, is struggling to save. When a crisis strikes — like unexpected job loss or a health crisis — there's no cushion. We all know too well how this played out during the COVID-19 pandemic. Salaries were cut. Jobs disappeared. EMIs didn't stop. Many learned the hard lesson that debt, without a plan B, is dangerous.

LESSONS FROM THE '90S

Money meant something different for older generations. More caution. Less debt. Some of their rituals may be worth reviving:

Need vs. Want — Just because you can, doesn't mean you should.

Save First — establish a reserve fund prior to taking a large loan

Beware of Breach — Look for hidden fees, variable interest rates, penalties — understand what you are signing up for.

Borrowing isn't the enemy. Bad borrowing is. Know the risks. Make informed choices. Make loans work for you, not vice versa

CONCLUSION

Loans make life easier. But they come with a cost.

If credit is used correctly, it can be a key. A home. A business. An education. But overuse? That's a trap. Debt piles up. Freedom shrinks. Future choices get limited.

Smart families find balance. They borrow only when it makes sense to, not because they're able to. They think beyond today. They would like to know: Am I going to beget this loan, or am I going to be enslaved to this loan?

Financial security does not mean that you have everything at this moment. It's about making choices that preserve options. Borrow with purpose. Spend with care. Build — don't burden.

Chapter 3

CULTURAL INFLUENCES ON SPENDING

In the context of India, culture plays a huge role in spending behavior, and there is a lot that can be written about this, so for this question, you can base your answer on what kind of impact traditions and culture (seen or felt) have on people's buying decisions. This chapter traces how the perfect cultural force pushes the young generation to spend (even though it doesn't make sense) Materials are not mere commodities in the home of ambi-pur lifestyles and Nexus phones undergoing transformations that revolve around traditional ideologies; it is a sign of standing among the masses. As a result, many young Indians put luxury before need, often letting their financial decisions be dictated by ingrained cultural values on status and appearances — factors that can both empower and burden them.

In the context of many facets of Indian culture that influence spending behavior, we explore the topic. Status symbols as part of aspirational living are at the heart of what you refer to as the social identity of the (inclusive/shared and exclusive/own categorizing) consumer goods that 'well-being or hyphenated happiness is to be found in the new symbolic meanwhile?' The chapter also monitors the effects of cultural gains and rituals, such as weddings and celebrations, where individuals are frequently pressured to overspend in the initiation of meeting societal expectations. It also investigates how advertising and marketing create our wants through culturally relevant storytelling and the overwhelming influence of peer pressure on our money. Acknowledging and contemplating these elements can potentially empower young adults in India to achieve a synthesis of cultural conservation and financial emancipation.

ASPIRATIONAL LIFESTYLES AND MATERIALISM

Aspirational living is so prevalent among young Indians, and that's in no small part due to our socioeconomic and cultural realities. At the heart of this lifestyle is the culture. The cultural value of things as status symbols and the need to own them drive this lifestyle. In India, ownership of certain brands of electronics, automobiles, or apparel is as much about consumption as it is about a fundamentally social identity. As such, for many young people, these things represent success, and they are a poignant indicator of who they are in society. The search for material wealth eventually leads to a whirlwind of wishes and wants – oh, how we stopped thinking about what we truly need.

Integrating these into our social contexts creates ambient social pressure, leading people to prioritize luxury over essential goods. Nigeria is a prime example of a country where the functionality of a product, such as a smartphone, may not be the differentiator for selection but rather the prestige derived from a particular brand. It is a scenario played out every day — from high-end gadgets versus budget offerings to branded tags versus unbranded attire. The need to feel that an individual has succeeded can outweigh dollars that could be spent on housing — or health care or savings — removing those funds from basic spending. Among aspirational cultures, stereotyping surrounds pressuring overspending to meet the standard. When the concept of hanging out is more akin to opening homes than the social spaces that are marketed as the new hot spot, when creative conversation about innovative ways to play and learn is on the verge of diminishing, and when business and our latest purchase dominate social conversation, it can be challenging to resist for an extended period. A consequence of this is that significant portions of income could be spent simply to demonstrate one mode of support or another, which offers little scope for rational fiscal management or planning for the future.

The aspirational living that ringleaders espouse can outshine lifelong frugality when it comes to extravagant events. Extravagance is the expected norm for birthdays, weddings, and anniversaries, even festive occasions. "When it comes to show-stopping events," the reader writes, young people "may drop thousands of dollars on an individual event and never think to curb the basic costs that allow them to live their life at all." For many, the joy of celebrating big outweighs the longer-term ramifications of excess. But culturally, these occasions can serve as a disruptive force to the economic legacies that young adults are attempting to establish without considering the frayed line between celebration and financial prudence.

If you can help others with realistic goals, it may reduce our need for stuff. Waiting to make nonessential purchases could help prevent impulse buying based on peer pressure, Lim says. If you can help others with realistic goals, it may reduce our need for stuff. As long as society encourages us to prioritize luxury, revising our personal Key Performance Indicators (KPIs) can shift our focus back to sustainability and meaning, rather than mere completion.

Moreover, aspirational cultures often encourage ideals that drive young people to overspend. By setting and adhering to a budget and confirming expense liability, one could eliminate unnecessary spending brought on by societal tendencies. It is here that creating customized budgets impacted by the unique situations they face becomes critical. You're trained to use simple but effective techniques, like the envelope budgeting system, to help you keep track of and control your spending without driving yourself crazy.

Bats require a luxury threshold, a need for luxury, and they are often the luxury of shit, but with low health canceling the most life; they are seen because they should be intermingled with the very first places of financial planning. It might develop discipline in financial dealings through these: It is important to practice mindful spending and saving. For instance, attending a seminar/workshop or reading educational material for personal finance serves as the first step up to financial literacy and leads you to the path of intelligent financial decisions!

Money is more than a means of survival. It's about status. In India, the spending habits aren't derived purely from logic — they are borne out of tradition, expectations, and image.

A car isn't just a vehicle. It's a statement. A wedding is more than a ceremony. It's proof of success. A designer handbag, a top-end phone — these are not just things. "They indicate belonging, achievement, and prestige.

Young Indians grow up seeing wealth as a mark of respect. Bigger homes. Flashier clothes. The latest gadgets are also available. Social media exacerbates this further — the comparison is relentless, and the pressure to "keep up" is eternal.

We prioritize luxury over necessity. That's the game. And many play it on credit.

THE WEDDING AND FESTIVAL EFFECT

Consumer spending doesn't end with individual desires. Festivals come with their own requirements: new clothes, presents, and banquets. Weddings? Weddings can lead to significant financial burdens. Families spend lakhs and even crows on extravagant celebrations. Weddings can be a financial storm.

In India, a simple wedding is considered a failure. In India, a simple wedding is considered a failure.

ADVERTISING AND PEER PRESSURE

But marketers know exactly how to sell. They exploit emotion, culture, and nostalgia. "This is gold for your daughter's future." "A real man drives this car." The message is simple — spend to conform, spend to be appreciated.

And if that weren't enough, there's peer pressure. A friend gets an iPhone. You need one too. Someone in your friend's group has booked a swanky hotel for a trip. Your weekend getaway seems suddenly small.

FINDING THE BALANCE

Spending isn't bad. The status isn't wrong. But when image trumps financial security, that is a problem.

Young adults need to pause. Am I buying this for me, or for what others think of me? Just that one question can alter spending behavior.

Real wealth does not lie in what you flaunt. It's what you keep.

THE COST OF ASPIRATIONAL LIVING

Young Indians are spending more than they have historically. They don't always do so out of necessity. This is often due to pressure.

Having the appropriate phone is essential. It's important to drive a car that meets your needs and preferences. These things signal success. Your smartphone is more than a phone. A car isn't just transport. They're status symbols.

I don't mean people buy things only for themselves. They purchase for the image they represent." The brand matters. The logo matters.

A ₹1,500 sneaker does the needful. But a ₹15,000 sneaker? That makes a statement. A ₹10,000 phone works fine. But a ₹1,00,000 iPhone? That puts you in a different class of athletes.

This urges to keep up traps many in debt. Monthly EMIs pile up. Credit cards get maxed. Savings disappear. However, there are still purchases to make.

No longer are social gatherings oriented solely around food and conversation. They're about what you own, what you wear, and what you drive.

Peer pressure is insidious and strong. If everyone in the group receives a phone upgrade, you can't help but feel enticed. If coworkers book luxury getaways, your budget trip seems suddenly small. The desire to keep up with others drives careless splurging.

TOO MANY CELEBRATIONS THAT COST TOO MUCH

Weddings. Festivals. Birthdays. Every occasion is a chance to display riches. The problem? Many go into debt to reach their potential.

A wedding that should be simple becomes a lavish one with a ₹30 lakh budget. A private birthday party becomes an event of social media spectacle.

These moments are fleeting. The expenses? They last for years.

Breaking the Cycle

The problem is not wanting nice things. It is a sacrifice of financial security for them.

A FEW STRAIGHTFORWARD ACTIONS CAN ALTER THE COURSE OF EVENTS.

Separate what you need from what you want. Just because something is in the zeitgeist doesn't mean you need it.

Delay major purchases. Give it a week. If the desire fades, it never matters.

Your compass, your definition of success Having money in your bank account beats a super expensive gadget.

Budget wisely. Try cash-based spending. When you do hand over money, you experience it physically.

THE REAL WEALTH

Success isn't how you dress, what you drive, or what you own. It's about what you keep. Being able to afford something is not the same thing as being able to keep it up.

The smartest people don't simply appear wealthy. They stay rich.

THE COMMERCIAL FOOD MAZE

The Grocery Store Trap

Walk into any supermarket. Shelves scream at you. "All Natural." "Superfood." "Protein-Enhanced." Buzzwords intended to get you to buy first, ask questions later.

In short, this product is superior. Healthier. Smarter.

Except, it's a lot of marketing bullshit.

THE ILLUSION OF HEALTHY

Turn the packet around. Examine the fine print. Sugars. Additives. Empty calories. The so-called "healthy" options frequently aren't much better than junk food.

Granola bars? Packed with sugar.

Flavored yogurt? Packed with artificial sweeteners.

Gluten-free snacks? These snacks are first and further processed than their regular counterparts.

You're paying a premium for a label, not better nutrition.

The Price of Taking the Hype at Face Value

This isn't just about food. It's about money and health.

Obesity is rising. The statistics are familiar: diabetes, heart disease, and lifestyle disorders are all on the rise. And yet at the same time, families are spending thousands on "premium" food products that provide nothing special.

BREAKING THE CYCLE

Know what you're paying for. Ignore flashy labels. Read the ingredients. If it's a long, unpronounceable list, back it goes.

Real food, in its simplest form, will always be cheaper — and healthier — than anything in fancy packaging.

THE "HEALTHIER" SNACK TRAP

The Healthy Snack Trap

Lisa, who is a mother of two, wanted healthier snack food for her kids. Something healthier. Less junk.

She brought home a box of granola bars from the store. "All Natural." "High in Fiber." The granola bars, coated in oats and honey, came in green, earth-tone packaging. It looked perfect.

Later, she checked the label.

12 grams of sugar per bar. That's three teaspoons. Palm oil. Artificial flavors. She wasn't buying healthy food. It was candy in disguise.

The Everyday Deception

Lisa's mistake isn't rare. It happens every single day. Consumers are charged more for food that looks healthy but isn't. Clever packaging. Misleading claims. Big price tags.

Granola bars. Low-fat yogurt. Multigrain chips. Organic cola. All sold as smart choices. Most aren't.

What's the fix?

Ignore the front of the box. Flip it over. Read the ingredients. Pick it up, and if there's too much sugar, oil or stuff you can't pronounce, put it back.

There is no fancy word necessary to describe real food. And it never had any hidden sugar in it.

THE GAME OF LABELS

Frontal Package Food Labeling: The Big Food Misdirection.

The food game contains a significant number of weasel words. They sound good. They sell better. But what do they really mean?

"All Natural"

What you believe: Fresh, healthy, chemical free.

What it actually means: No artificial ingredients — but lots of high-fructose corn syrup and preservatives.

"Superfood"

What it's called: Vitamin-rich and nutrient-dense.

What it actually means: a buzzword sans legal definition.

"Protein-Enhanced"

What you do: Protein will be useful for energy and the building of muscle.

What it typically means: More protein, high in sugar and fats.

The Protein Shake Scam

One popular meal replacement shake contains 20 grams of protein. Sounds great, right?

Look closer. 42 grams of sugar are present. This is more than a can of soda.

THE TRUE PRICE OF BEING TAKEN IN BY THE SPIN

Breaking It Down

Financial Costs

Overhyped "healthy" snacks: ₹250 per serving

Whole food alternatives (nuts, fruit): ₹125 per serving

That extra ₹125 adds up fast. Spend ₹1,500 more per month? That's ₹18,000 a year — for food that's often less nutritious.

Health Costs

Sweetened "health" foods? Linked to obesity, diabetes, and heart disease.

India already struggles with rising lifestyle diseases.

Medical expenses for diabetes and heart issues? Can wipe out savings.

Fake foods don't just hurt your wallet. They hurt your body too.

HEALTH COSTS:

The Hidden Cost of "Health" Food

Most so-called "healthy" foods are loaded with sugar. Granola bars, flavored yogurts, and protein shakes claim to be good for you but fuel obesity, diabetes, and heart disease instead.

The Price of Poor Health

In the U.S., healthcare costs linked to obesity top $173 billion annually. India isn't far behind. Medical bills for diabetes and heart conditions are skyrocketing.

The Burden on Low-Income Families

Families already struggling financially spend extra on "healthy" products. They believe they're making the right choice.

But these products are often more expensive and less nutritious than simple, whole foods. The result? The outcome is a reduction in income and a decline in health. It's challenging to break free from this trap.

FIGHTING BACK

Breaking Through the Noise

Read the Labels

Ignore the fancy packaging. Skip the buzzwords. Flip the box over.

Avoid added sugar, excessive salt and unfamiliar ingredients. If it resembles a chemistry experiment, turn it around.

Know What Matters

Some words are regulated. "Organic" has standards.

Others? "Superfood" means nothing. It's just marketing.

Choose Real Food

Whole Foods wins every time. Fruits, nuts, vegetables and grains don't require ostentatious labels.

They are less expensive, have more food, and have no surprises.

Push for Change

Demand clear labeling. Champion food policies that prioritize health over profit.

No one should pay to learn the truth.

THE BIGGER PROBLEM

Why does this keep happening? Money.

In 2023, food companies spent over ₹1 lakh crore on marketing. Their goal? Make you believe that their "healthy" products are worth the upcharge.

Or take a ₹500 bottle of "cold-pressed superfood juice." Now imagine a fresh orange for ₹10. The difference? Pure marketing.

The Real Cost

The real question is not about health. The real question is not about health.

And it's about profiting from the illusion of health.

Families like Lisa's bear the financial burden. They bear the consequences not only in financial terms but also in terms of their future health. They believe they are making the right decisions. They aren't.

What Can We Do?

Stay informed. Read beyond the labels.

Shop smart. Lifestyle Change: Whole Foods Over Hype

Demand better. Stronger food regulations. Clearer labeling.

The more quickly we stop believing marketing tricks, the more quickly we reclaim our health.

CULTURAL INFLUENCE OF CELEBRATIONS AND RITUALS

The Cost of Celebration

Spending culture shapes. In India, it does so in big, expensive ways.

Weddings. Festivals Naming ceremonies. Every moment is a declaration, not only a celebration. How much you spend matters. Your event's outward appearance matters more, even.

Social Status vs Financial Reality

For many families, celebrations don't have to be personal. They're public performances. It's just another way to show status, earn respect, and establish social standing.

A simple wedding? Considered embarrassing. A modest Diwali? Searches which read financial deficit

So, families stretch. Savings disappear. Loans pile up. And debt becomes a thing of custom.

THE WEDDING TRAP

Weddings are the most egregious examples. They are not merely a union—they are an extravaganza.

Film stars host extravagant parties. Luxury is glorified on social media. The pressure trickles down. Even middle-class families find themselves trying to emulate a millionaire's lifestyle for a few days.

Multi-day events. Designer outfits. Exotic venues. Recovering from a week of celebration can take years.

Festivals That Empty Pockets

Diwali. Navratri. Durga Puja. Every occasion brings gifts, banquets, adornments, and competition.

The joy is real. So is the financial strain.

Entire neighborhoods compete to have the best-dressed house. Families are pressured to spend more, give bigger, and celebrate louder.

THE HIDDEN COST OF KEEPING UP

Cities amplify that pressure. Society watches. Relatives comment. This often leads to spending beyond one's means being a social necessity.

Many feel trapped. They desire to reduce expenses, yet they dread criticism. You know, the burden of expectation is far too heavy compared to the financial logic.

Breaking the Cycle

It wasn't a contest to spend more. A wedding is a celebration, a festival, a milestone; it should be joyous, not poverty-making.

A few shifts can make a difference:

Establish a budget before emotions overwhelm you. Tradition does not have to be expensive.

Skip the competition. Bigger isn't always better. Smarter spending is.

Tell genuine joy apart from social obligation. A significant celebration doesn't have to come with an extravagant price tag.

Teach financial awareness. A generation brought up on spending will not exactly be good at saving.

A grand affair runs for a couple of days. The debt lasts for years. It is a time to reflect on what is important.

CHANGING TASTES: FROM HOME-COOKED MEALS TO ONLINE ORDERS

A Shift in Eating Habits

From Home-Cooked to App-Ordered

In the 1990s, the kitchen was the heart of every Indian home.

The food was fresh, home-cooked, and shared. Mothers planned meals. Families ate together. Eating out? Eating out is a rare treat. This treat is specifically reserved for special occasions such as birthdays, anniversaries, or Sunday outings.

Today? A different story.

Swiggy, Zomato, and the Click-to-Eat Culture food delivery apps changed everything. No planning. No cooking. Just tap, pay, and eat.

Dining out isn't an event anymore. It's a habit. People often do it on credit.

The Price of Convenience

This shift isn't just about food. It's about money. It's about health.

Ordering in means higher bills, extra charges, and impulse spending. A single meal costs twice or thrice what home-cooked food would.

The impact? Wallets shrink. Waistlines expand.

A Lifestyle, not a Necessity

Eating out used to be occasional. Now, it's routine.

Cafés are workspaces. Food courts are hangout spots. Weekend dining is non-negotiable.

The result? The result is a culture characterized by excessive spending, excessive eating, and insufficient saving.

Time to Rethink the Plate

Cook more. Order less. Convenience isn't worth financial stress.

Set a food budget. Treats should feel like treats.

Think before tapping 'Order Now'. Is it hunger or habit? The duration of the meal is only a few minutes.

But financial habits last a lifetime.

THE CONVENIENCE TRAP

The Convenience Trade-Off

Cooking takes time. People are busy. Something had to give.

Home-cooked food still rules in its own way in Indian households. Now? Takeout and fast food and delivery apps have come rushing in.

A SMALL CHOICE, A BIG COST

The idea of not eating in the kitchen seems harmless enough. There may be one meal here and another there. But the habit sticks.

The result? Higher expenses. Poorer health.

Fast food is not just for the body. It drains the wallet too.

THE HIDDEN PRICE OF CONVENIENCE

Making meals from scratch is less expensive than dining out. Yet many still choose the costlier path.

First, it's just to save time. Soon, it becomes routine.

Monthly food bills shoot up. Savings shrink. Waistlines expand.

RETHINKING THE KITCHEN

Home cooking is more than food. It's about how well you can control what you eat and how much you spend.

2,000 of monthly costs avoided with 1/8 of a man-month of upfront planning effort.

Simple meals can be easy, healthy, inexpensive.

Eating out was never meant to be an addiction.

The choice is simple. You can choose to enjoy yourself now or make

SCENARIO 1: RESTAURANT VS. HOME COOKING

The Convenience Trade-Off

Cooking takes time. People are busy. Something had to give.

Home-cooked food was once a staple in Indian households. Now? Takeout, fast food, and delivery apps have become increasingly popular.

A Small Choice, A Big Cost

The no-eating-in-the-kitchen rule seems harmless enough. There may be one meal here and another there. But the habit sticks.

The result? Higher expenses. Poorer health.

That is not only how fast food affects the body. It drains the wallet too.

The Hidden Price of Convenience

The Cost of Eating Out

Consider a typical family of four living in Mumbai, for instance.

Dining Out:

One dinner at a mid-range restaurant: ₹1,500 per person.

Eating out thrice a week: ₹1,500 × 3 × 4 (weeks) = ₹18,000 in a month.

Cooking at Home:

You can make the same meal at home for just ₹300.

Total monthly cost: 300 x 3 x 4 = 3,600 per month.

The Difference? A Huge Savings Gap.

One saving ₹18000 − ₹3600 = ₹14400 per month.

That's a savings of ₹1,72,800 every year. This amount is sufficient to fund a vacation, make investments, or cover a year's worth of school fees.

A minor shift — massive financial effect.

CREDIT CARDS: THE WIND IN THE SAIL

The Credit Card Trap

Swiping a card feels easy. Too easy. No cash. There is no need for hesitation.

The pain? The pain comes later—through interest, late fees, and ballooning debt.

Meet Raj: A Case Study of Pricey Convenience

Raj, 28, works in marketing. He loves food delivery. It's fast, easy, and always a few taps away.

He spends ₹10,000 on Swiggy every month. But he does so with a credit card.

Initially, it feels manageable. Then the interest kicks in.

If your ₹10,000 balance accrues 36% at an annual interest rate, you owe ₹13,600 in a year—simply for paying the minimum due.

How Food Delivery Apps Clean Out Your Wallet

It's not only the cost of the food. It's the maneuvers they use to get you to spend more.

Flamboyant promotions turn excess ordering into a deal.

Minimum thresholds for "free delivery" that squeeze you into buying more.

Time-limited offers a fake urgency.

No order seems like a terrible deal. But you figure out eventually who's built the thing in the end.

The Fix? Spend Smart.

Pay using debit cards or UPI instead of credits. It makes spending feel real.

Limit monthly food deliveries. Stick to it.

Ask yourself—do you need this meal, or is it force of habit?"

Because convenience shouldn't be a drain on financial freedom.

SCENARIO 2: ORDERING IN VS. COOKING IN

The Cost of Convenience

Online Ordering:

One meal: ₹250 (including delivery).

Two times a day for 20 days: ₹250 × 2 × 20 = ₹10,000 a month.

Eating Out:

The daily food cost: ₹90.

Eating outside for 30 days: ₹90 × 30 = ₹2,700 per month.

Cooking at Home:

One meal: ₹50.

20 days of home-cooked meals: ₹50 × 2 × 20 = ₹2,000 a month.

The Hidden Loss

Food delivery is an extra ₹8,000 a month as compared to home cooking.

That's ₹96,000 per year — almost a lakh spent on overpriced, app-ordered food.

What Can You Do with That Money?

Invest it.

Save for a vacation.

Pay off debt.

The choice is simple. As far as convenience is concerned, it shouldn't cost you your financial future.

EATING OUT AND THE HEALTH COSTS EATING OUT AND THE HEALTH COSTS

The Hidden Cost of Eating Out

Not just your finances are affected. Your health pays too.

Restaurant food and fast food are drenched in oil, sugar and salt. Regular use causes obesity, diabetes and heart disease.

And poor health? It was expensive.

Ramesh's Story

Ramesh, 35, an I.T. professional, enjoyed dining out. Fast food was easy. Cheap. Quick.

Then came the test results. High cholesterol. The doctor warned him. Dedicate yourself to serious changes in your life or face a lifetime of medication.

Now, he pays ₹2,500 every month to doctors and for medicines. That's ₹30,000 per annum — simply to take care of his health.

A CYCLE THAT KEEPS TAKING

First, you pay for the food.

Then you pay for your health.

Finally, you pay for the treatment.

The solution? There should be an increase in home-cooked meals. There are fewer takeout orders.

In real life, savings don't merely materialize in your bank account. They happen in your body too. The Hidden Cost of Eating Out

It's not just your wallet that suffers. Your health pays too.

Meals at restaurants and fast food are heavy on oil, sugar, and salt. But when consumed regularly, you will end up with obesity, diabetes, and heart disease.

And poor health? It was expensive.

THE PAST IS PROLOGUE: WHY EATING IN MATTERS

Lessons from the '90s

Life was simpler. So was eating.

Affordable Food Choices

Rice, dal, and vegetables were the staples that formed the basis of each meal. Healthy. Filling. Cheap. The cost is a fraction of the restaurant prices.

Healthier Meals

Cooking at home, we knew what went into our food. There were no hidden oils present in our food. There is no added sugar.

Family Time

Dinner was more than a meal. It was a daily ritual. Conversations took place around the table, not via a delivery app.

Finding the Right Balance

Eating out isn't the problem. Overdoing it is.

Meal Prep - Cook in batches. It prevents you from ordering takeout.

Make Dining Out Special — Save it for real occasions, not laziness.

Set a budget — Determine how much you will allocate for restaurants per month. Stick to it.

Use Credit Wisely – Using credit to pay for basic food? Bad idea. Reserve credit for emergencies, not just cravings.

Food serves as more than just fuel and sustenance. It is about how much agency you have over your health and money.

THE TAKEAWAY: COOK FOR YOUR WALLET AND YOUR HEALTH

The Hidden Cost of Convenience Eating out isn't just about food anymore. It's a lifestyle shift. It involves a shift in time.

Cooking at home feels like effort. Ordering in feels easy. But is that easy? You pay for it.

You first make the payment with your wallet. Next, consider the impact on your health.

THE VALUE OF HOME COOKING

Home-cooked meals save money, cut unnecessary calories, and bring families together. This is a simple habit that yields long-term benefits.

Less spending. More control. Fewer health risks. Stronger connections.

A SMALL SHIFT, A BIG IMPACT

You don't need to quit restaurants. Just reduce the habit.

Cook one extra meal a week.

Eat out for occasions, not convenience.

See food as fuel, not entertainment.

THE TAKEAWAY

Happiness doesn't come from takeout boxes. It comes from balance.

A little planning, a few home-cooked meals, and a shift in mindset — that's all it takes.

ADVERTISING, MARKETING, AND PEER INFLUENCE

The Way Culture Influences Spending in India

India straddles tradition and modernity. It's a combination that works for marketing.

Ads don't just sell products. They sell feelings, belongings, and dreams. They weave in family values, festival traditions, and success stories. The goal? Turn the act of spending into something that feels intimate, requisite — ennobling.

Marketing That Doesn't Feel Like Marketing

Think of the ads you see.

A father passing a gold chain to his daughter and saying, "This is for your future."

This type of festive feast everyone laughing, the previous message ear mouth smile — "A little product or different genres are also how many celebrate, celebrate the brand."

A young man in a sharp suit, holding out the latest phone — "Success looks like this.

These aren't just promotions. They are stories designed to get you to buy.

Pressure to Keep Up

And pressure is everywhere for young Indians.

Friends upgrade their phones. Coworkers eat at the hippest cafes. Influential figures on social media lead lavish lifestyles. Feeling like you're falling behind is a common experience.

Most spend merely keeping up. This is true even when their bank accounts reveal a different story.

THE HIDDEN COST OF BELONGING

Your new phone could thrill you for a month. A designer bag might catch eyes for a week. But the EMI? It lingers.

Marketers know this. They promote the lifestyle, not the price. And people buy it — over and over.

TAKING BACK CONTROL

Question the pitch. Is this product valuable or in status?

Separate needs from wants. Just because it looks good on someone else doesn't mean you need it.

Talk about money. Normalize telling people, "That's not in my budget this month."

Being wise with money doesn't mean deprivation. It's more about owning your choices — not letting marketing or peer pressure do that for you.

CULTURAL ACCEPTANCE AND IMPACT OF BORROWING

How Culture Influences Spending Behavior in India

India combines tradition with modern aspirations. This is the fuel of marketing.

Ads don't just sell products. They peddle feelings, community, and aspiration. They link family values, festival traditions, and stories of accomplishment. The goal? Make purchases seem personal, essential — even noble.

Marketing That Sounds Like Culture

Think of the ads you see.

A father placing a gold chain into his daughter's hand, telling her, "This is for your future.

A fun-filled meal that brings everyone together and everyone laughing, the message of course is simple — "Celebrate with our brand."

A young man in a sharp suit, holding up the hottest new phone — "Success looks like this.

These aren't just promotions. They are stories designed to get you to purchase.

PRESSURE TO KEEP UP

The pressure on young Indians is coming at them from all sides.

Friends upgrade their phones. And co-workers eat at the trendiest cafés. On social media, influencers bask in luxury. You may feel as though you're falling behind.

Most are spending simply to keep up. Despite the discrepancies in their bank accounts, they continue to spend.

The Hidden Cost of Belonging

A new phone may wow you for a month. A designer bag might catch the eye for a week. But the EMI? It lingers.

Marketers know this. They sell the lifestyle, not the expense. And people believe it — over and over.

Taking Back Control

Question the pitch. Are you adding value or simply status with this product?

Separate needs from wants. Just because it looks great on another person doesn't mean you need it."

Talk about money. Practice saying, "That's not in my budget this month."

Curbing spending isn't the same as denying yourself. Making sure you get what you want and what you pay for without marketing or peer pressure is key.

INSIGHTS AND IMPLICATIONS

Culture and Money: Always a Push and Pull

This chapter looked at the intersection of culture and finances in India.

Young people balance hopes and expectations. Success is not just about earning, it's about proving it. A good car, a good phone, a good designer label — status symbols are important.

But the pursuit of appearances has its price. Debt. Stress. People rely on their paychecks for their livelihood. Breaking the cycle is a challenging task.

THE COST OF TRADITION

Weddings, religious rituals, and festivals — big splurging is the norm. Families spend life savings on grander events that often blow their wallets.

There is a collision between tradition and financial reality. And sometimes, reality loses.

FINDING THE BALANCE

Celebrating culture doesn't have to come with financial hardship.

Set limits. Be traditional but within your limits.

Challenge the norm. A fancy wedding is not the only measure of happiness.

Talk about money. Silence perpetuates negative financial behaviors.

Spending culture shapes. However, financial wisdom determines the future.

Chapter 4

COMPARING INDIA'S FINANCIAL HABITS

Refinancing isn't merely a financial strategy; it's a reflection of how various culture's view debt. Do not forget, loans are tools in the U.S., designed to be tweaked, renegotiated, and made optimal. In India, debt is a contract, a promise to be kept rather than rescheduled. These radically different mindsets lead to dramatically different approaches by borrowers to meet their obligations.

In America, refinancing is second nature. Homeowners exchange low mortgage rates for higher ones. Credit card debt gets consolidated for more manageable payments. Credit card debt is often moved to better deals. It's simple logic—lower interest, improve cash flow, maximize spending power. It's a cycle that keeps cash flowing. For some, it's a savvy financial move. For some, it's a snare that results in life-long repayments.

But this is India, and things are different here. A home loan is more than a financial transaction; it's an obligation for a lifetime. Changing terms mid-way? Rare. Even when there are better alternatives, most borrowers pause. It is preferable to take more risks, and for the time being, the choice is to continue incurring financial losses. Banks don't aggressively promote refinancing, and many people don't even know that it is an option. Stability takes precedence over flexibility.

Why the gap? There are three keys (well, details, if you want). The first is mindset — Americans view debt as a tool, whereas Indians think of debt as a burden. The second is market evolution — the U.S. financial system is designed to facilitate constant debt restructuring, while India's is still emerging. With risk appetite — Americans will play financial maneuvers, but Indians are much more circumspect.

For young borrowers, the takeaway is simple. Refinancing is a good tool, but it's not always the right one. There may be hidden fees with lower rates. A straight loan might be preferable to one that changes its spots. Financial security is the aim, but the means to that end differ.

LESSONS FROM THE AMERICAN AND INDIAN GREAT RECESSION: THE DEBT TRAP

The Great American Recession caused eight million lost jobs from 2007 to 2009. Foreclosures claimed over four million homes. Was the dramatic rise in household debt in the years leading up to the recession in the United States coincidental? Absolutely not. American households' total debt shot up to a staggering $14 trillion from $7 trillion 2000-2007, a sure sign that the system had been gorging on credit and was bloated with a sub-prime proportion of debt.

In the past, the turns of economic downturn like the Great Recession and the Great Depression were preceded by an exponential growth of household debt and subsequently a staggering drop in consumer spending. If the banking crisis has received public attention, research and data point to the conclusion that government policies have been too focused on saving (or bailing out) banks and creditors and too little on tackling the underlying problem — over-indebtedness of households.

One misunderstanding is that a rise in the flow of credit is the ultimate tool in stabilizing a crisis-hit economy. But if the real problem is too much debt in the first place, flooding the system with new credit merely compounds it. When household debt is excessive, you have foreclosures, and people cut spending and save." A decline in consumer spending lowers demand for goods and services, which reduces production and leads to massive job losses — a vicious cycle that keeps economies trapped in prolonged stagnation.

THE 2007–2009 INDIAN ECONOMIC SLOWDOWN: ANOTHER TRAJECTORY

While the U.S. struggled with a severe recession driven by household debt and the instability of the financial sector, India experienced a slowdown that didn't blossom into a full-blown recession. During that time, the economy in India was stagnant, and GDP growth went down from 9.3% in 2007 to 6.7% in 2008-09. But India did not experience as deep an economic contraction as the U.S. because of important structural differences.

In contrast to the heavily leveraged consumer credit in the American economy, India's financial system was significantly less susceptible to subprime lending. Personal debt levels among Indian households were lower, and mortgage penetration had far less reach. The Indian banking sector, under the leadership of the Reserve Bank of India (RBI) enforced rigorous lending expectations, averting a housing market bubble spawning similar to that of the U.S.

But India was not entirely insulated from the turmoil that engulfed global financial markets. The stock markets crashed as the Sensex fell more than 50% from early 2008 to early 2009. Slowed exports from lower global demand affected sectors like IT, textiles, and manufacturing and resulted in job losses — though not to the extent seen in the U.S.

To spur growth, the Indian government responded with fiscal stimulus, including higher infrastructure spending and tax cuts. The RBI has also executed monetary policy easing—cutting interest rates and guaranteeing liquidity in the banking system. These measures in time enabled India to recover more quickly, with economic growth bouncing back to 8.5% by 2010.

LESSONS FOR THE FUTURE

Simple lessons can be learned from the Great Recession and the Indian slowdown: economies with excessive consumer debt are vulnerable to financial disasters, while those with prudent banking policies and diversified growth drivers can withstand global shocks more effectively. The U.S. experience serves as a cautionary tale against the evils of unrestricted borrowing, whereas India's tenacity emphasizes the significance of regulating it and practicing fiscal prudence.

For India, the (mis)lead is to keep tightening financial regulations even as growth continues to become increasingly dependent upon external conditions. We must examine financial policies around the globe and build on our mistakes to invest generously in our economic futures.

DIFFERENCES IN REFINANCING PRACTICES

The first and most visceral difference between India and the U.S. in their financial habits is refinancing. Refinancing is a financial move American citizens are looking for. And many Americans view this as a chance to reset their financial plans in ways that can pay off handsomely. When interest rates fall, for instance, homeowners tend to rush to refinance their mortgages. In doing so, they're paying a smaller monthly amount and freeing that cash flow up for other financial goals, like retirement or more education.

In the U.S., refinancing is about more than just lower interest rates. It is also commonly used as a debt consolidation tool. If you have a mountain of high-interest credit card debts to balance, then you can feel a bit overwhelmed. ### THE ANSWER: REFINANCING Refinancing is a way to solve a problem; it brings together many loans into one big loan, usually with a lower interest rate. This streamlining not only reduces stress — it empowers people to regain control over their financial conditions. It enables them to chart their long-term plans with a clearer sense of their financial obligations."

As it happens, there's another bit of dynamic refinancing in America that makes it alluring: Home equity lines are another appealing aspect of refinancing in America. Homeowners have years and years of unassessed wealth sitting on their books because we assess the value of real estate.

Refinancing allows us to access this equity, which we can use to fund major purchases like home improvements, business startups, or higher education. This resource eliminates the need to create another way to spend money that won't enhance Americans' overall quality of life. We keep this type of acquisition very conservative, as it enables substantial purchases without depleting current savings or assets.

In India, the perspective on refinancing is entirely different.

Here, refinancing is approached more cautiously, and the practice is less common. Most Indians perceive refinancing as a pocket-sized list rather than an opportunity for financial optimization. Several cultural and economic factors contributing to this hesitance influence financial decision-making.

Indians have been extremely averse to debt traditionally. The cultural context emphasizes financial restraint — and, at times, saving overspending. As a result, many are avoiding practices that could put someone further in debt, such as refinancing. That, as well as the limited refinancing options available in India, unlike the U.S., has created a situation where financial institutions are less willing to serve borrowers, where they should be, and eliminate lifetime borrowers.

The contrast between these two countries, in the ways refinancing operates in practice and its status in mind, mirrors other divides in their respective financial cultures. Whatever surplus we build is old school money making, any emergent debt incurred by the explosive expansion of the economy is long term debt India is still flooded with this classical mindset, which always infixes the shipment payments as a result, most Indians seem to rely on available financing options, whether it's refinancing or using up savings to cover an economic emergency.

To understand the differences in attitudes, one must delve into the cultural background. This is, however, tempered slightly by the fact that Americans have faith in their finances thanks to debt management and education programs about them that have become common from an early age. II. Moreover, stiff competition among financial service providers in the US has further resulted in attractive refinancing options for consumers and encouraged the refinancing shopping trend.

However, the infiltration of money into India's social psyche has been less seamless. Younger generations, who are increasingly valuing financial independence, are changing this, but old money habits persist. Many Indian families thus receive advice at home (what is termed "double wound"), rather than from such service providers — the strategy implies continuing dependence on the traditional ways and suspicion over other mainstream financial tools, such as re- refinancing.

UNDERSTANDING FIRST—THE U.S. VS. INDIA—A TALE OF TWO FINANCIAL MINDSETS: REFINANCING

In the U.S., refinancing is a widely used financial tool, whereas in India it is still an underused concept. Why? The disparity can be attributed to culture, financial habits, and market structures.

If Americans view refinancing as the best option, Indians tend to be more cautious and often favor savings over debt restructuring. Let's examine why these attitudes exist and how they manifest as financial behaviors in both countries.

HOW TO REFINANCE AND OTHER U.S. FINANCIAL STRATEGIES: NOT LAST RESORT

In the U.S., refinancing is not only an option; it's a strategy. Whether it's a mortgage, a student loan, or credit card debt, refinancing is often viewed to reduce costs, allow for more cash flow, or consolidate debt.

- Lowering Interest Rates – Homeowners flock to refinance their homes when interest rates go down. A lower rate acts like lower monthly payments, leaving them the extra cash for other priorities like retirement savings, investing, or education.

- Debt Consolidation – Got high-interest credit card debt? Many people in America choose to refinance their loans to consolidate multiple loans into one loan, often with a lower interest rate. This makes managing finances much easier and reduces stress monthly.

- Accessing Home Equity – As property prices surge, homeowners often access home equity to finance significant expenses such as home renovations, launching a business, or college tuition. This strategy enables them to make large purchases without touching savings.

Basically, refinancing is perceived in the U.S. as merely a method to better one's finances, not to force someone to show their financial cards.

WHY INDIANS DESIST FROM REFINANCING: A CULTURAL PERSPECTIVE

Refinancing is much less common in India, and when it does occur, people typically view it with suspicion. The financial and cultural habit of debt avoidance embeds this reluctance.

- Debt Aversion & Financial Conservatism – A lot of Indians prefer to save rather than borrow. Even assuming better terms on a loan, taking on more debt is considered risky or unnecessary.

- Less Refinancing Choices – In the U.S., banks actively market refinancing in their portfolio, whereas, in India, financial institutions provide fewer options, and depositors face stringent eligibility conditions.

- Reliance on Family & Traditional Financial Planning — In lieu of refinancing, a vast majority of Indian households rely on family savings or informal loans to fulfill their financing needs. This long-built habit tends to make people shy away from structured financial instruments.

- Financial Ignorance – In the U.S., financial literacy is taught at a young age, with schools and corporations providing debt management courses. India also has a nascent financial literacy ecosystem, which means refinancing may not even be in the system for many consumers.

THE TIPPING POINT: IS IT TIME FOR REFINANCING IN INDIA?

India's Financial Landscape Changing with Globalization Younger professionals are generally more receptive to tools like refinancing, as are those exposed to international markets.

Fintech is democratizing loan restructuring and refinancing.

Disposable incomes are growing, and with it comes a desire to explore debt management options beyond the conventional ways.

And global exposure is changing mindsets as well, as professionals working or studying abroad export their financial habits homeward, such as refinancing.

Refinancing won't completely supplant India's savings-first mentality overnight but is likely to become more mainstream in the years ahead.

CONCLUSION: TWO WORLDS, TWO WAYS

Refinancing in the U.S. can be seen as a financial flexibility and optimization tool.

Second, debt is commonly viewed in India as a thing that should not be restructured but reduced.

There is merit in both approaches, but as India's financial markets develop, it may start to come to terms with (or see the benefit of) refinancing as a viable strategy — just as the U.S. gradually has. The enablers will be consumer education, accessibility, and a cultural shift around debt.

CREDIT CARD USAGE DISPARITIES

When researching personal finance, you will come across many elements of finance, one being credit card usage, especially in the US and India. Credit cards, likewise, have become something so entrenched in many Americans' daily lives, interactive as many people are with the day-to-day for their rewards programs, perks like travel points or cash back, and assistance with building and sustaining a good credit history. Additionally, credit cards rely on a robust infrastructure of financial literacy that begins in childhood and education, enabling the reasonable extension of credit. American consumers already have a kind of education for credit card use because they know they have to pay down their balances each month to avoid mind-staggering, huge (some might say predatory) interest charges and that they have to pay interest so that they learn how to manage credit responsibly and carefully to build their credit scores.

For a lot of young people in America, credit cards are their first taste of financial independence. They discover how to balance obligations against income and pay for daily expenses sensibly. However, rewards structures incentivize spending not only on general purchases but also in specific categories such as dining, groceries, and travel, thereby maximizing the accumulation of points and increasing the use of credit cards in everyday transactions. So, they're garnering some long-term perks, like higher credit scores and more negotiating power for better credit later in life.

This is much more circumscribed than credit card use in India, which is also growing. There has long been a cultural aversion to debt, which has transformed into a preference for the stocking of possessions rather than their loaning. Until recently, many Indians shied away from credit cards and preferred cash or debit cards that they traditionally mistrusted out of fear that they could become trapped in a cycle of unpayable debt. However, this reluctance is gradually changing as younger demographics increasingly align with international consumer trends and embrace electronic payment processing.

However, this budding romance between the Indian youth and card ownership has a huge mismatch in their understanding of how credit cards work — primarily payment mechanics.

While their American peers may learn from an early age how to manage credit, many young cardholders in India have little idea about interest rates, billing cycles, or the consequences of making minimum payments.

Even working people strive to show up towards a standard and compromise a lot with their own origin by spending a lot on clothing, etc.; thus, this adds fuel to the already burning plight of the young sections of society. There is this tension between the seductiveness of modern finance and the rigid norms of frugality and savings. While credit becomes more accessible to these users, the necessity of strong financial education and guidance is also on the rise to make sure they can use their credit responsibly and avoid the dangers associated with credit usage.

In this environment, advice for enhancing matters remains relevant. Now, we need more such financial literacy programs in India for youth. You know, schools and financial institutions are in such a position to affect lives by putting together a holistic workshop, seminar, and course approach that makes personal finance manageable. These programs could start with the basics, such as budgeting, terms of credit, financial goals.

Indian banks and financial institutions offering easy-to-use resources, such as education apps or online calculators, on what responsible usage of credit entails would also help. Other features that send users alerts in real time when they're approaching a spending limit, a payment, or a potential fee may benefit users as they try to navigate the complexities that come with credit. Combined with a reward-based incentive model, similar to the rewards systems set up in the U.S. for responsible credit behavior, they could promote responsible spending.

Credit cards are nearly unavoidable in the United States, used for purchases at grocery stores and travel and in all manner of other situations — often as a means of accumulating rewards points and managing cash flow, but also a method of establishing a credit history. But in India, there has historically been a strong cultural aversion to debt. While credit card usage is on the rise, some opt to use cash or debit cards instead, so they do not get into financial trouble.

FROM THE U. S.: CREDIT CARDS AS FINANCIAL TOOL

Most Americans learn about credit cards in high school or college. The system of financial literacy in the U.S. is structured so that many young adults realize that:

- Using credit responsibly means that you must pay off your credit card balances each month to avoid incurring steep interest.

- The importance of credit scores—which factor into everything from loans to renting an apartment—is crucial.

- How to maximize it — cash back, travel points or markdowns on your regular purchases.

Credit cards aren't just about spending; they're also about strategy. Americans use them to:

Debt consolidation — transferring high-interest balances to lower-rate cards.

Urgent buys — when savings fall short.

Cash-flow management involves borrowing money to buy something while the investments appreciate.

For a financially literate person, a credit card is less a debt trap than a financial asset.

THE CREDIT LANDSCAPE IS CHANGING IN INDIA

In India, credit card adoption is much more restricted. Traditionally, people have favored saving over borrowing, viewing credit as a warning sign.

However, things are changing. Younger generations — conditioned to a life of global consumerism, digital banking, and fintech innovations — are much more comfortable juggling credit cards. Yet, a knowledge gap remains.

There are many first-time users of credit cards in India.

- They lack knowledge about interest rates and billing cycles.

- Do NOT assume that if you make a bare-minimum payment, you're safe from being in debt.

- Unbalance between expenditure and incoming leading to financial pressure

Add social pressure to that, and it is one deepening problem. Young professionals often feel the need to project a certain lifestyle — travel, dining, shopping — even if they cannot really afford it. Without understanding how to use credit responsibly, this can quickly lead to unmanageable amounts of debt.

Let Your Money Work for You: Financial Literacy and Credit Usage**

Financial literacy programs also need to adapt to prevent consumers from overextending credit in irresponsible ways in India. Schools, banks, and fintech platforms can help in a few ways:

- Setting up schools and colleges' credit management classes.

- Provide interactive tools — like apps and calculators — to show the true cost of credit.

- Users will receive alerts from the system when a spending threshold or an impending due date approach.

- Rewards for good credit behavior (like cashback and travel points in the U.S.)

Rich talk about credit, as promoted by money experts, influencers or even local people you trust, might help demystify credit cards and de-stigmatize responsible use.

BOTTOM LINE: ONE MINDSET, TWO METHODS, ONE DIRECTION

In the U.S., credit cards pervade financial culture, with education and consumer-friendly policies creating dynamics that benefit providers and borrowers alike.

Credit card usage is increasing in India, but it requires some adjustment.

The task ahead will be education, awareness and responsible financial behavior — need driven from making credit cards viewed as an enabling financial tool rather than a debt trap — as India begins to make the move to a credit-friendlier economy

THE GROWING PARALLELS IN LOAN-DRIVEN LIFESTYLES

The truth is globalization is changing personal finance everywhere — and the difference between the way Indians and Americans think about loans is an extreme example of foreign financing absorption. There is much to consider when it comes to altering borrowing patterns, considering both the historical context and ongoing changes in those two nations.

Well, post-Second World War, historically, in the United States, we thought of loans as a possible means for economic development to the extent that you could own them. A true consumer society started to emerge then, centered around a burgeoning middle class with greater purchasing power than ever before. Loans, in turn, supported financing for all kinds of goods and services, from housing to education to cars and beyond, bolstering a culture that at least justified going into debt as a path toward the American Dream. And of course, the postwar economic boom was fueled by massive government programs such as the GI Bill, which helped veterans buy homes and go to school, but it wasn't just the package that spurred economic growth — it set a template for avoiding notice and capturing the latent economic bounty tapped by debt.

In the U.S., consumers, seeking a better quality of life without having to wait for savings to purchase costly goods, quickly adopted this practice. The widespread acceptance of consumer credit as a normal way of life underpins this practice.

So it was with India, as well, where a craving for modern appliances accompanies upwardly mobile middle-class life. Given that most larger retailers offer attractive financing deals, it is reasonable to assume that most households can afford these items through affordable installment payments. It stands to reason, then, that, although these two countries began with different starting points, consumers in both places behave much the same today in terms of how they charge their purchases. However, this reliance on loans carries a hidden cost, which becomes apparent only when you understand the concept of vehicle financing. It's a common practice to enable personal transportation, particularly in India and the U.S., where the allure of unending investment is strong. Vehicle EMIs, insurance premiums, and maintenance costs can significantly impact household budgets. In fact, these obligations leave both nomadic and non-nomadic borrowers financially hostage: they live too much in the red, highlighting the need for a budget, and especially one regarding debt.

If we comprehend all of this, we should perceive loans as merely an option, not as a resource. Responsible borrowing means being aware of the risk that the borrower bestows, such as the interest rate, and how the borrower's decisions affect the market and how to properly hedge that risk so that you take advantage of opportunities without committing a fraudulent credit decision. You are fueled with the "foreignization" data till 2023, October

Being a smart financial person means, in part, knowing when else to refine. We're going educational about the intricacies of making that refinance (lowering interest rates and one debt pays off the other – what helps the borrower is what puts the scale back in balance) and continuing to turn content to the borrower that empowers their decision and is in best practice for their total financial position. Teaching young adults, including college students and graduates, how to make informed decisions about debt management is crucial in enabling them to take control of their financial futures. If they are aware of their situation and focus on the problem, they can make their own plans based on their needs and the facts to take advantage of globalization's opportunities and avoid its dangers.

FROM PUBLIC TRANSPORT TO PRIVATE DEBT — THE PRICE OF 21ST-CENTURY TRAVEL HABITS

A Trip Down Memory Lane

Most of urban India in the 1990s was cheap and simple to travel in. Most people relied on buses, trains and shared autos as their usual transport choices. Having a car was a distant dream, only attained after years of hard saving and poverty after divorce. Air travel? That was an emergency or special occasion, a rare, NOT an everyday thing

Now fast forward to today, and all this has changed. Later it was cars — cars and ride-hailing apps such as Ola and Uber — that took the place of public transport. Flying is an ordinary feature of life — ordinary features in credit cards and loans. Though the changes have made things easier, they've also come at a steep price for many.

HOW THE MOVE FROM SAVINGS TO PER EMIS BROUGHT OWNERSHIP OF VEHICLES

Back then, families saved for years to purchase a scooter or bike, which lasted for decades. Now, every one of the household may own their own bike or car — usually purchased through equated monthly installments (EMIs).

FOR INSTANCE, SCENARIO 1: TWO-WHEELER VS PUBLIC TRANSPORT

Buying a Bike – Ravi, a collegegoer in Bengaluru buys a bike worth ₹1.2 lakhs on a two-year EMI plan at 10% interest. He spends ₹5,550/month for a total lifetime expenditure of ₹1.33 lakhs (2 years).

Public Transport: Ravi spends ₹1,500 on a monthly bus pass. Over two years, that's ₹36,000; nearly ₹1 lakh less than if he had bought a bike.

RIDE-HAILING APPS: NEWFOUND CONVENIENCE COMES AT A COST

Ola and Uber can cater to your commuting needs, albeit at a higher cost. They're often pricier than public transport and, in some cases, even personal cars.

How the Transformation from Savings to Per EMIs Narrated Vehicle Ownership

Families would save for years to afford a scooter or bike, which they would use for decades. Now each household member owns separate bike or car — Generally through EMIs.

For example, Scenario 1: Two-Wheeler & Public Transport

Purchase of a bike – Ravi, a collegegoer in Bengaluru purchases a bike costing ₹1.2 lakhs on a two-year EMI plan at 10% interest. ₹5,550/month, ₹1.33 lakhs (2 years) total spent.

Transportation: Ravi pays ₹1,500 for his monthly bus pass. That's ₹36,000 over two years; almost a ₹1 lakh less than if he'd purchased a bike.

UBER AND LYFT: NEW CONVENIENCE OF RIDES HAS A PRICE

Ola and Uber are at your disposal to cater to your commuting requirements but only at a higher price. They're often more expensive than public transport and, in some instances, personal cars.

SCENARIO 2: UBER VS PUBLIC TRANSPORT COMMUTE

Uber: Neha, who works out of Delhi, spends ₹400 per day on her 10 km commute to the office via Uber. That costs 8,000 a month or ₹96,000 a year.

Her monthly travel expenses by Delhi Metro: ₹2,500 (₹2,500 x 12 = ₹30,000). She saves ₹66,000 annually.

But air travel is apparently our new normal, with costs obscured.

Air travel used to be a privilege or at least an inconvenience; now it's routine for a lot of people — one they often buy with a credit card. But the interest adds up quickly when dues are partially paid.

SCENARIO #3 LIMIT YOUR FLYING/VS TRAIN TRAVEL

Flying: A family of four booked round-trip tickets from Mumbai to Goa at ₹8,000 each, crossing out ₹32,000. The person is two eligible for a credit card — where one pays interest at 3% a month; and six months down, the cost is ₹40,000.

By train: If the same journey was taken by train in AC 3-tier, the entire family would have spent ₹6,000, thereby saving ₹26,000.

Hey, go-getters: The True Cost of Private Vehicles to General Society

The cost of a vehicle isn't limited to the purchase price. There are costs for fuel, insurance, maintenance, and parking.

SCENARIO 4: CAR VS PUBLIC TRANSPORT

Car: Amit buys a car for ₹ 8 lakhs on a five-year loan at eight percent. His EMI (Equated Monthly Installment) towards the loan works out to ₹16,500, ₹10,000 towards fuel and maintenance, and ₹10,000 a month, overall, ₹26,500 a month. He builds ₹5.1 lakhs in 5 years = ₹5.1 lakhs.

(₹2,000 train pass, saving ₹14.7 lakhs by spending ₹ 1.2 lakhs for five years)

The Ripple Effect of Private Travel

The switch from public transport to private vehicles and air travel has ramifications:

Increased Expenses: Not much to save or invest after monthly EMIs or credit cards.

Cause for Concern: Cars are the only increasing quantity; with cars come no more walks or bicycles; hence, more lifestyle diseases.

Environmental impact: No cars, air travel and air travel all worsen pollution and climate change.

LESSONS FROM THE PAST

The travel trends of the 1990s provide some important lessons:

Public Transport: Cheap, enviro-friendly and fast.

You know your history: do you really need that vehicle loan?

Smart Travel: Skip charge cards for discretionary spending and budget-cap flights

The First Word: Satisfaction

Private vehicles and air travel have made life much easier (or at least pretended to) but chained most of them to long-term economic bankruptcy. Is it worth it?

This chapter goes on to explain the premises that small and planned actions—for instance, taking the bus instead of an Uber or opting out of unnecessary EMIs—compound into considerable savings, in terms of not just money but also health and eco-impact. Therefore, let's refrain from excessive spending and prioritize managing our debt.

WHEN ESCAPES BECOME BOUGIE: ROUTING THE BANK ON TRAVEL HABITS

Vacations: Then and Now

Vacations were straightforward and cheap in the 1990s. My father organized family outings to the homes of acquaintances, visits to towns and shrines where the majority of our family were born, and patterned short vacations around places with cultural or spiritual significance. It was all about hanging out together without spending a ton of money.

These days, vacations are grander, more elaborate, and—occasionally—international. Millennials envision travel among palm trees in Paris, Bali, or Dubai, equipped with five-star hotels and business-class tickets. But these trips frequently come with a price tag — financial security — as many are paid for with credit cards or personal loans.

Traveling Abroad — on Your Credit Card

Travel loans and simple EMIs have made global vacations possible for several middle-class families. Convenience often comes with long-term financial anxiety.

SCENARIO 1: DOMESTIC GETAWAY VS. INTERNATIONAL ESCAPE

Scenario 1: Domestic getaway vs. international escape

Old-School Holiday: A family of four travels by train to Jaipur, stays in a simple guesthouse, spends ₹10,000 for a week's travel, stays and eats there

Now Dubai Trip is Present Day: The same family spends ₹30,000 (per person) on airfare, ₹10,000 (per night) on a hotel, and ₹20,000 on activities. The total is ₹2,00,000, paid with a credit card. Considering the rest of the amount gets 36% compound interest per year, the actual cost of ₹7,00,000 — paying just 5% of the total amount (₹34,999) as the minimum due — comes around to ₹2,72,000 for a year.

THE COST OF AWESOME PRICES FOR FLIGHTS

Air travel has become the default for vacations, rather than the occasional luxury. Throw in luxury hotels, and a quick trip can turn into an expensive undertaking.

SCENARIO 2: RAIL VERSUS AIR TRAVEL FOR A FAMILY VACATION

This same family spends ₹6,000 on a round-trip AC 3-tier train journey from Mumbai to Goa.

Air: ₹24,000 for the same route (tour flights) There, a three-night stay at a luxury resort costs ₹45,000, taking it to ₹69,000.

Budget Solution Staying in a guesthouse for ₹3,000 a night and taking the train saves ₹45,000

SOCIAL MEDIA: THE PRESSURE TO SPEND

Social media has heightened their desire for exotic holidays. Their desire for exotic holidays has been heightened by social media. Posting aspirational photos from far-off locales seems to be a prerequisite, which is why so many people are dedicating their lives to pursuing it.

Example:

Riya, a 28-year-old software engineer, was now stuck with a week in the Maldives, which she had booked for ₹3 lakhs through a personal loan. The equated monthly installment (EMI) was ₹15,000 for the next two years, which left her with no chance of saving or investing. The vacation brought her likes on Instagram, but the debt remained long after the holiday cheer wore off.

THE UNSEEN COSTS OF DEBT-FUELED TRAVEL

Debt-financed vacations may feel amazing at the time, but they usually have some nasty outcomes:

Higher EMI: More Debt = Less disposable income for other necessities.

Missed goals: Savings toward a home, education, or retirement are neglected.

The toll on emotion: Financial stress can generate family tension and mental fatigue.

Lessons from the Past

The 1990s taught us so much about how to keep vacations affordable and meaningful:

Travel Within Your Means: An undiscriminating trip will do just as well for golden memories.

Sounds Local: Consider places you don't have to finance.

Earn, Then Spend: Save up for vacations rather than putting those expenses on credit.

MAINTAINING A SAFE ONLINE PRESENCE WHEN TRAVELING

Set A Budget: Know how much you can spend without going into debt.

Travel When It's Off-Peak: Look for deals when traffic is lighter.

Stay Smart: opt for homestays, guesthouses or Airbnb instead of luxury hotels.

Build Up: Start a vacation savings account.

CONCLUSION : MAKE MEMORIES, NOT DEBT.

Vacations should be joyful, not financially stressful. While international trips and five-star stays are exciting, they do not necessarily translate into happiness. Simple, mindful travel can be just as gratifying — without the baggage of debt.

So, this chapter serves as a reminder to us that enjoyment comes from experiences, not extravagance. Ensure planning wisely, allocate funds wisely, and create lasting memories that surpass an EMI.

CULTURAL AND PSYCHOLOGICAL DRIVERS OF LOAN CULTURE

For a loan, the amount of loans in India and who pays them off must be questioned since the nation, religion, or game cannot repay them. We have many money habits by default, dictated by what society expects of us. Neighborhoods in India, where social class is vital, encourage individuals to borrow money even when they can manage without it simply to protect their social status and check family obligations. Neighborhoods in India, where social class is vital, encourage individuals to borrow money even when they can manage without it simply to protect their social status and check family obligations.

It even incorporates spending on weddings, festivals, or other socially important events. Borrowing is similarly a social necessity in the U.S. There is significant social pressure as we strive to maintain our status as upper middle-class individuals by purchasing homes in desirable neighborhoods and enrolling our children in prestigious schools.

With social media streaming in unfiltered images of life, good and bad, the pressure to appear stable has only heightened. The showcases of people's days on platforms like Instagram and Facebook can feel like cyberspace coliseums, and people judge whether their lives stand up to what they read on everyone else's profile, which only intensifies the already-real craving to be on par with their peers." In this instance, the effect plays out in the growing number of individuals borrowing items such as travel, gadgets, and apparel to emulate aspirational lifestyles showcased on social networks, experts say. Ruining Lives in the USA: social media promotes consumerism in the USA and lures people to swipe their credit cards and personal loans for similar happiness.

Over the last few years, India and America have mostly gone from avoiding method-facing debt to more code-facing debt acceptance.

Indian culture traditionally values saving and discourages debt; it views borrowing as a final option. However, due to economic liberalization and easier access to credit facilities, debt has become a fundamental aspect of life for the younger generation. And the same goes for the U.S. by a long explanation, even though there is always a greater borrowing factor; the fact is that there are normalized and ramped-up debts caught by at least one sort of debit, whether student loans, mortgages, or credit cards.

This reframing reflects wider cultural swings, in which debt is not inherently a subject to be dreaded by all in polite conversation but instead a utilitarian means to achieve a financial end. For example, in India, borrowing for education or business is now a righteous act, consistent with aspirations for upward mobility. Conversely, in the U.S., the myth of debt serving as a tool to enhance living standards and secure financial investments against future growth is deeply ingrained.

The emotion that you felt having to take on a debt — having to meet needs or having to meet wants — is all vastly different, and it has serious mental health implications. When borrowing is for needed expenses — as, say, medical bills or tuition — the stress involved in going into debt is generally counterbalanced by a clear, return-on-investment-style payoff. But when borrowing goes toward fulfilling wants rather than need to fund vacations or buy luxury goods — the subsequent indebtedness can provoke guilt, regret, and anxiety about repayment.

This further makes borrowing even for non-essential reasons a mental trauma for many in India which results in such stigma to persevere." In one extreme example, young professionals, burdened with mortgages and other debt, attempt to live as independently wealthy as possible, only to find themselves torn by family members' demands and the internal tension between their personal dreams and the need to pay their bills every month. In the United States — a country where consuming, by way of credit, is so popular it's colloquially known as "buy now pay later" — debt can carry an emotional toll and introduce problems and strains on mental health, especially when borrowers go beyond their means of repayment and into delinquency.

IMPACT OF LOANS ON FINANCIAL STABILITY

While they can provide relief from financial difficulties, excessive reliance on loans can pose a risk. In either India or the USA, loans have become a must-have part of one's personal finance. But while they do lead to short-term financial help, leaning too heavily on them can become a long-term source of financial dependence, creating a cycle of touching debt that can be impossible to break. It can be difficult to repay these loans when people are taking out more than they can afford. This vicious circle not only provides terrain for the lockdown of financial incomes but also engages in a savings perspective for the future.

Many individuals have a lot of stress and anxiety in their lives due to their ongoing debt obligations that cause harm to their mental health. In India, as in the U.S., avoid feeling inundated by one's bills, which can lead to stress-related illnesses. Individuals do not bear the emotional toll alone; it extends to entire families. Be warned: the pressure to miss bill deadlines and for people to make monthly payments will get into households and destroy relations and family structure! It is important to know the seriousness of these psychological consequences when developing healthier financial habits.

Whether or not a person will overspend or manage debt responsibly is, in part, a matter of teaching them to borrow wisely. Programs on financial literacy that target young adults — including college students or recent graduates — can assist these young adults with understanding how to make an informed decision about taking out a loan. Such lessons about budgeting, interest rates, and credit terms, while basic, can empower consumers to determine whether they truly need a loan or have alternatives. Familiarity with the different loan types, interest rates, and repayment plans can help you avoid borrowing based on impulse due to societal pressure or any temporary acquiescence to your taste.

Building credit systems and sound financial behaviors is a substantial factor in avoiding debt. To deter them from its path, lenders must focus not on quick, easy approvals but on why borrowers can repay their respective debts. As a borrower, habits such as saving regularly, setting financial goals, and understanding credit scores that will help you in the long term are some of the things you can work on developing. Credit systems underpinned by a baseline of transparency and accountability will better serve people and families.

Therefore, marketing lending integrations with practices of responsible credit use can help. Understanding the whys and when taking a loan out, learning just how powerful timely payments can be, and being aware of the terms that come with it are many ways you can avoid falling into many of the pitfalls. This fosters a mindset that views loans as a tool to enhance one's financial power, rather than as a burden that could potentially diminish it.

"Financial institutions must play an active role in educating their customers on how to prudently use loans and associated financial products. Guideposts for managing monthly payments — and planning for longer-term financial health — can shift the way people think and behave about debt. This could involve personalized financial training or seminars about informed financing decisions.

Also key is the cultural change necessary to normalize conversations about money, debt, and financial health. Referring early to someone close or bringing attention to the issue often normalizes the discussion, enabling individuals to seek help without feeling ashamed. Whether community forums, educational seminars, or professional counseling services, such conversations about financial well-being can open more intentional conversations around borrowing and spending practices.

Moreover, comparing these trends in both India and the U.S. provides additional context. There are nuances, such as different societal norms and more disparate economic landscapes, but the reliance on loans and the strain resulting from financial stress are similar in both regions. The youngest are the best positioned to show the path to better, more sustainable, and growth-oriented financing systems through the sharing of lessons learned from successes and failures.

When included as components of financial education and public policy, these features could form a basis for the future of loans in both countries as a tool to convert opportunities into leverage, possibly without putting anyone's economic stability at risk. Regular education and financing in person will have as much budget for environmental sustainability and become household and individual economic habits.

SUMMARY AND REFLECTIONS

This chapter discussed the opposing financial behaviors of India and the United States, with our focus primarily on refinancing. Could it be that, while Americans generally consider refinancing a strategic means to tune their financial plans (be it mortgage refinancing or debt consolidation) Indians tread with caution? The contrast derives from cultural values emphasizing frugality and restraint in expenditure in India, where debt is generally considered a last resort. By contrast, the U.S. provides a wealth of refinancing choices underpinned by nascent financial coaching, presenting refinancing as a frequent means of managing personal finances. We use a lens that puts these differences in a larger cultural and economic context at a time when both countries may continue to change how they do things because of globalization and technology. This helps to bridge the gaps between their different ways of thinking.

So, these financial habits offer a few insights, especially for young adults, college students, and graduates with little clue of how to navigate the world of finance today. In this landscape, the Indian youth find themselves caught between the traditional investment wisdom and the allure of 21st-century financial instruments. Given the growth of fintech innovations and improved financial literacy, there is potential for change in the perception of refinancing and use of credit. At the same time, drawing lessons from American experience regarding the value of financial literacy and judicious borrowing could help the next generation in India. Equipped with these fundamental teachings, young readers can lay the groundwork for a secure financial future, empowering them to navigate a financially evolving landscape with informed decision-making skills.

Chapter 5

LIFESTYLE TRENDS AFFECTING FINANCES

LIFESTYLE CHOICES & FINANCES: YOUR DAILY DECISIONS AND WHAT THEY MEAN FOR YOUR WALLET

We often don't notice it, but lifestyle trends influence our spending habits, usually in ways that are either subtle or more apparent. Social norms, peer influence, and convenience shape what we choose to eat when we go out, where we travel, how we shop, and what we decide to do on the weekend, even where we choose to live. And even if these choices aren't harmful in the moment, they can make a big difference in long-term financial security.

And the effect is even more powerful for college students and recent graduates. Newfound independence, social pressures, and media exposure to aspirational lifestyles (thanks, social media) can lead to spending patterns that don't necessarily align with financial goals. This chapter examines the ways that lifestyle choices—both major and minor—impact financial success and how to create harmony between living well and living within your means.

WHAT LIFESTYLE TRENDS MEAN FOR SPENDING

Let's break it down. Here are some top ways finances are affected by modern lifestyle choices:

- Eating Out vs. Cooking at Home

  Dining out is more than a matter of convenience — it's frequently a social occasion. Meeting friends for brunch, ordering takeout after a tough day, or making regular coffee runs might seem innocent enough. But overtime? It adds up. It may seem like nominal expenses can wipe thousands from your budget every year.

- Social Media Pressure on Luxury Travel

  Vacations have made travel a status symbol. "Work hard, travel harder" is nice in theory — until you're stuck paying off credit card debt from a trip you couldn't truly afford. Go on vacations that are financially realistic and affordable to avoid putting yourself in a stressful, money hole.

- Home Buying & Car Purchasing – Need Vs. Want

  For the majority, owning a home and a car feels like the mark of success. But is it always necessary?

  Homeownership: The soaring prices of real estate have made homeownership an expensive target, and renting is not necessarily a bad financial decision.

  Expense Number 3) Car Ownership: A lot of people take out a loan to pay for their car, and while that car can seem like a blessing, there are expenses far beyond that loan, such as fuel, insurance, and maintenance. If that works for you, public transport might be a better way to go.

- Subscription Services & "Little" Luxuries

  From streaming services to gym memberships to premium apps, subscription-based spending has exploded. The problem? Payments are automatic, and we don't often think about how much we're spending. Reviewing these expenses on a regular basis can ultimately help reduce unnecessary costs.

STRIKING A BALANCE: FINANCIALLY SMART, NOT DEPRIVED

The aim isn't to stop all spending it, it's to be thoughtful about how you spend it. Here's how to have fun in a financially responsible way:

- Determine what you plan to spend money on: If travel is a priority for you, cut back on other discretionary spending.

- Never Fall for Lifestyle Creep: Earning more doesn't mean spending more.

- Use social media cautiously: inspiration can be useful — but don't let it dictate your financial decisions.

- Reassess "Needs" vs. "Wants": Is that luxury apartment worth an extra stretch in your budget, or will a less fancy place suffice?

Knowing how lifestyle choices affect finances is the first step toward making better decisions. The trick is moderation — savoring the now without compromising financial stability later.

SPENDING BEHAVIORS LINKED TO DINING OUT

Dining out has Hidden Costs Pretty Much Your Daily Choice Will Affect Your Wallet

Many of us, especially young adults and college students with busy schedules, have become accustomed to eating out, whether it's cooking late at night or going out to eat. A quick bite between classes, a weekend brunch with friends, or the occasional late-night takeout at the time never seems like such a big deal. But over weeks and months? All those meals are a drain, both on the purse and health.

For many, going out to eat is not just about food — it is about laissez faire, socializing, and sometimes even status. But by grasping the real cost of this habit, you can make better decisions without giving up your enjoyment or taste.

The Hidden Price of Eating Out

A meal at a restaurant or two or three food delivery orders here and there might not sound substantial, but let's do some math:

A ₹300 coffee and snack combo every alternate day? That's ₹4,500 a month.

Ordering takeout twice a week at ₹500 per meal? Another ₹4,000 gone.

Two nights out with friends for ₹1,200 a night? Simple ₹10,000+ by month end

You may be unknowingly spending ₹15,000–₹20,000 per month just on food. You could use that money for savings, travel, or student loan repayment.

And it's about more than money. Health is another cost we bear. Restaurant foods are typically loaded with salt, sugar, and unhealthy fats, which can lead to long-term health problems. The ease of eating out is not without its indirect costs — not only to your bottom line but to your health.

Why We Won't Stop Spending: The Social & Psychological Pull of Getting Meals Out

Dining out is as much a social activity for many young adults as it is about eating. It's about reconnecting with friends, toasting small victories, or simply getting a break from the drudgery of home-cooked meals. And to be clear, there's also the power of social media.

It makes it hard to resist spending outside of your planned budget to try the next viral trend hot spot, be it a café or a restaurant.

Friends are always making plans and FOMO (fear of missing out) makes it difficult to say no.

There is also lifestyle pressure that reinforces the notion that dining out often is a measure of success and sophistication.

While there's nothing wrong with eating out every now and then, it's become a habit you feel obligated to do because of someone else.

Balancing Enjoyment & Financial Awareness

So how do you enjoy eating out without destroying your budget? Being intentional is the key. Here are some ways to find a balance:

- Allocate a Dining Out Budget: Figure out a reasonable extravagance on restaurants for a month and stick with it. If you are eating out four times a week, cut it back to twice.

- Select Experiences Versus Frequency: Rather than spending time on meals here and there, save for a singular dining experience that feels deserving.

- Discover Clever Alternatives: Enjoy restaurants for the ease? Are you planning to prepare a small weekly meal to avoid ordering takeout at the last minute? Enjoy the social aspect? Skip dining out and instead host a potluck or cook a meal with friends.

- Keep a Record of Your Spending: Use a spreadsheet or an app to determine how much you're spending on food — you may be surprised.

Cooking at home doesn't need to be dull or lengthy. You can start enjoying this activity and save thousands of rupees every year. Also, you can control the ingredients, making it a healthier choice than restaurant food.

The Bigger Picture: Of Dining Out and Your Financial Future

Small spending habits have long-lasting impacts on students and young professionals who aren't settled in their careers and aren't financially stable yet. That ₹20,000 a month on eating out? It could have been:

- An emergency fund for unforeseen expenses

- Savings toward a dream trip rather than a one-off meal

- A course, or an investment in your future

This isn't about never going to restaurants or denying oneself social experiences. It's about the considerations we make that align with our financial goals. So, you can still enjoy great food — without jeopardizing your future financial security — by being more mindful about where and when you spend time.

VACATIONS AND THE RISE OF LUXURY TRAVEL

Why Luxury Travel Is on the Rise, but Should You Pay the Price?

Travel is not what it once was. Once upon a time, vacations were uncomplicated—road trips to visit relatives, cheap holidays, or a weekend in a nearby city, all on a shoestring. Now? Travel has turned into a circus.

As a result of social media, and Instagram particularly, the nature of a "good" vacation has changed. Now, a soothing getaway isn't sufficient. Now, it's overwater bungalows in the Maldives, helicopter rides over Dubai, and Michelin-starred dining in Paris. And though these luxury getaways may lead to some beautiful photographs, they also have an expensive price tag — a price tag that many don't fully think through until it's too late.

The Social Media Effect: Inspirations to Travel vs. Bankrupt Travel

Swipe through endless reels of influencers sipping cocktails in Santorini or lounging in infinity pools, and it's easy to feel FOMO — that old feeling of missing out. But what do we don't see? Brand sponsorships, gifted stays or, you know, the actual amount of debt some people accrue to finance these fantasy vacations.

And for young adults — particularly those who are new to a career or juggling student debt — staying up with that culture of luxury travel can be a dangerous financial proposition.

Airfare, lodging, meals, and excursions can all add up quickly. Even a "quick" weekend trip can quickly balloon into thousands of rupees.

Luxury travel creates a trap of spending. Once you experience a five-star resort, you can't go back to budget hostels or economy flights.

Opportunity cost matters. Every ₹10,000 spent on a trip is ₹10,000 that could have been saved, invested, or used to pay off debt.

This does not imply that you should never travel. It just means that travel should be within your financial reality — not an idealized version of it.

Budget Travel: An Alternative You'll Still Find Luxurious

However, those who enjoy exploring without exceeding their budget can still opt for budget-friendly travel. And it doesn't necessarily mean sacrificing fun or comfort — it just requires a different mindset.

- Plan smarter, not pricier. Traveling off-season, utilizing credit card reward points, and booking accommodation well in advance can all reduce costs considerably.

- Think beyond fancy hotels. Splurging on a cozy Airbnb, a boutique hostel, or even an overnight train rather than a flight can release funds for better experiences.

- Experience in aesthetics. You also don't have to stay in a luxury suite to appreciate the beauty of a destination. Skip fine dining and private chauffeurs and choose street food, local cafes, and public transport instead.

- Create a travel budget you can stick to. Generalize before you book: How much can you afford without dipping into savings or maxing out a credit card?

When you travel on purpose, rather than traveling on impulse, you can create wonderful adventures without jeopardizing your money.

THE TAKEAWAY: APPROVAL OF CONTEXT TRAVEL

It can be tempting to fall into the "travel now, worry later" way of thinking, especially when it seems like everyone else is living their best life within an airport lounge. But your financial well-being should always come first.

For cash-strapped students and young professionals weighing the costs of debt, growing their careers, and saving money, the tradeoffs that come with indulging in luxury travel are something they should be familiar with. So rather than pursuing Instagram vacations, pay attention to what really matters—memorable experiences, prudent expenses, and monetary independence. Ultimately, the value of peace of mind surpasses that of any five-star retreat.

APARTMENTS AND MORTGAGES: THE RISING COST OF MODERN LIVING

Housing trends still greatly impact financial behavior with both a new graduate and millennial entering the workforce. You know, metropolitan housing stocks often feel like a mountain to climb, and only hilltop getting that will be surgery, right? Home prices are going up, and each day is a closer step to owning a taste of the American dream. That trend, largely the result of rapid population growth and development in those areas—was driven in part by strong demand for housing that pushed prices up in the small number of homes for sale. That is why they then lie on the remaining credit that often lasts for years just to apply to live.

Home loans can help when you want to buy property, but they also serve as a long-term financial obligation that can significantly affect your financial situation. The excitement that comes with identifying a property and the pain that comes with structuring deals can overshadow decades of repayment schedules that become affixed to such properties — in some cases for as long as 30 years. Such loans consume a significant portion of monthly income, making retirement savings and other essentials feel less important during the probationary period. With time, that borrowed money's hall-of-mirrors compulsion may not only siphon disposable income but also slow down other more financially liberating objectives, such as work, investments, or retirement savings plans. Nor is this cultural mandate that encourages people to flaunt wealth through real estate just about trading up to a better home. The impulse sometimes spills over into larger expenditures on furniture and lifestyle enhancements that seem to connote whatever prestige the home conveys. These costs, individually small, add up overtime and could collectively have a second impact on your budget. This demonstrates the importance of realism over ambition, as homes reflect a range of financial situations, not just social classes, which hold greater value.

These hidden costs of homeownership play a crucial role in accurately assessing the cost of purchasing a home. While focusing on the price listed on a sign in the window of a house you've eyed is certainly the simplest way to approach the home-buying process, homeownership is complex, with costs that extend well beyond the price tag. Repair and maintenance work in and around the house is among the perennial worries for homeowners — maybe an annual bill, which could come to add up quickly depending on how old or ramshackle the house is. Routine repairs — plumbing or dishwashers, say — or sudden problems — a leaky roof, structural damage — may require immediate — and often expensive — attention."

However, the steady accumulation of ownership costs in a home also includes property taxes, homeowner association fees (for certain complexes), insurance premiums, and utility bills. When inflation, property value, etc., improve, these costs will increase as well — making your financial plan more complex. If you plan to purchase a house, whether it's a single-family house or a condo, it's crucial to conduct thorough research and calculate the associated costs, as house ownership entails numerous expenses.

SMART SHOPPING: THINGS TO KNOW WHEN YOU'RE YOUNG

For recent graduates and young professionals, the decision-making process to purchase a house should be rooted in financial reality rather than societal expectation. If you're thinking about a mortgage, here are a few points to consider:

- The Size of the Loan: When taking a loan, always make sure you know what the interest rates, loan tenure, and commitment to repay it are.

- Know What the Government Is Doing: Governments in several countries announce programs to assist first-time home buyers that may be able to ease the financial burden.

- Rent Vs Buy: Renting is not wasting money if you could save, invest, and stay flexible. A mortgage is a long commitment; not everyone should jump into a marriage like that.

- Expand Your Search Area: Scouting a little farther away from all the places you'd want to live can help reduce housing costs quite a bit without sacrificing the quality of life.

- Live Within Your Means: A house is an asset, not a burden. Avoid the option that will set you up for glory.

THE TAKEAWAY: STATUS SYMBOLS OF SMART HOMEOWNERSHIP

Owning a home is a big milestone — and it's not a race. The consequences of getting a mortgage without a full understanding of what you are getting into can drag you on a decades-long road of financial stress.

As for young adults who feel pressure to buy, my best advice would be a philosophy of how to make (good) money, not social norms. Having a house is a beneficial investment if it doesn't cost the freedom of your finances.

VEHICLES AS NECESSITIES: THE FINANCIAL STRAIN OF MODERN M

With the world's rapid urbanization, owning a personal vehicle has become increasingly tempting for average Indian young adults and recent graduates. However, this tendency carries a significant cost, as it can lead to financial instability. Given that, as a rule, none of our country's cities have sufficient public transport infrastructure to meet the needs of their soaring populations, this unhealthy correlation encourages people to drive. Picture living in a metropolitan area, where, instead of reaching your destination in half an hour, your commute time becomes an hour and a half longer due to taking a train, bus, or tram. Obviously, most of the city's working populace, which directly correlates with the number of active students, are not willing to lose an hour's sleep every day and are under time constraints. Which is why this factor of necessity, or rather perceived necessity, when there is no human alternative—bad train or overcrowded bus—is hard to attribute to the term needed when it comes to choosing a legal way to get around. Yet, opting for a personal vehicle brings the heftiest price. Naturally, acquiring a set of wheels means not only spending money on the initial purchase. Often, taking out a car loan becomes an additional factor in one's financial demise. On paper, car loans may not seem like a significant financial burden. However, when combined with personal vehicle insurance, all accommodation costs, and other expenses, a car loan becomes a financial asset. On paper, car loans may not seem like a significant financial burden.

In addition, outside of the car sticker price and the monthly loan repayments, there are ongoing costs that prospective vehicle owners must think about. Recurring costs such as maintenance, insurance, and fuel prices can significantly impact a budget. While regular maintenance is vital to head off more expensive repairs later, it can still surprise many first-time car owners in terms of how often service is needed and how much it can cost. Compulsory or comprehensive insurance adds another layer of expense. It is a matter of cost that does not change but rather guarantees protection against loss, but for that, its own rates and premiums, most opposing, will depend on the car model, age, and driver's history.

Fuel prices are constantly fluctuating, adding to the cost. Whether it's an increase in oil prices on the international market or changes in local policies, these fluctuations directly impact drivers' petrol prices, often causing disruption to even the most well-laid plans. Even during weeks when gas prices remain stable, the rising frequency of long-distance commutes due to urban sprawl can significantly increase the frequency of weekly trips to the supermarket and significantly increase monthly expenses.

So, if owning a vehicle means paying at least for all these costs, then why do fresh graduates or young adults still flock to possessions? Largely, it's a question of social pressure and ambition. For many, owning a vehicle is a symbol of success and independence, particularly for those freshly entering adulthood or taking their first steps in their career. But there's a built-in prestige to driving your own car, amplified by social media portrayals and peer comparisons.

And there are things you can do to ease financial pressure. Never purchase a vehicle without consulting in depth on the total cost of ownership. This requires looking beyond the monthly installment and interest rate on the car loan to the annual costs associated with maintenance, insurance, and fueling. Wise budgeting and worshipping can help individuals determine whether to own one without affecting other spending priorities. Otherwise, using a carpool, ride-sharing services, or choosing an economical model can provide some respite from high spending. It's also worth exploring the public transport routes and timings — particularly if it would eventually expand its offerings. Navigating lifestyle and budget through planning and understanding.

IS HAVING A CAR: A NEED OR A FINANCIAL BURDEN?

Buying a car is a significant milestone for many young adults, symbolizing independence, demonstrating success, and providing a practical mode of transportation. Who wouldn't want to zoom through crowded urban streets in their own vehicle, rather than waiting for a stuffy bus or delayed subway?

But here's the thing: A car isn't just the car you buy. It is a laundry list of hidden costs that can surreptitiously suck your money. Before you sign on the dotted line on that loan agreement or before you upgrade to that shiny new model, however, you might consider asking: Do I really need this, or am I merely keeping up with the Joneses?

IS IT REALLY WORTH IT? THE SOCIAL PRESSURE TO HAVE A CAR

It's not just a matter of convenience — there's a status to having your own car. It's a status symbol in many cultures — a sign of having made it as an adult. "What it needs a car for when it has social media and friends, and a car may not be the smartest financial decision as well."

The public transport infrastructure in India is still far from ideal. Train delays are a common occurrence, buses frequently lack sufficient seating, and the absence of a reliable timetable can make traveling from point A to point B a challenging process.

However, driving is still fun, and like healthcare, automotive engineering is an expensive must-have if the less the better at some level of performance.

Maintenance Life But the reality is messier. It might not be the wisest call financially, particularly when starting out in your career, to own a car. Like so many things, price is only part of the story. But the bigger burden begins with their overhead — loans and insurance, fuel and maintenance, and even unexpected repairs — which can quickly eat up any savings that you might have worked hard to accumulate.

The Cost of Driving: What You May Not Factor in Your Car Ownership Budget

Having a good amount of buying power is good when you want to take out a car to finance it, but that's not where it ends. It entails a tangle of ongoing expenses that many first-time buyers fail to anticipate.

♦   Loan Payments & Interest

Many young buyers will be financing their cars, meaning they'll sign up for years of monthly payments. A loan may look manageable on paper. With interest rates, the real cost may be much higher than the vehicle's price.

♦ Maintenance & Repairs

Purchasing a car necessitates ongoing maintenance. Servicing, oil and tire changes, repairs, etc., all contribute to periodically draining your wallet. Skipping maintenance can result in repairs becoming significantly costlier down the line.

♦ Gas Prices: Constant Expense

Fuel prices fluctuate. They drop from time to time, but mostly they go up — leaving car owners racing to adjust plans for spending. A long daily commute? That's just more pressure on wallets.' *

♦ Insurance & Taxes

Car insurance is required by law, and comprehensive policies can be surprisingly expensive depending on car model, age, and driver history. And then there is the purchase price and the registration fees for road taxes.

♦ Parking & Toll Fees

In big cities, parking is expensive and scarce. Factor in tolls for long commutes, and suddenly, your "affordable" car becomes a bottomless pit of expense.

Here's your real-world math: Too many car buyers do not consider these ongoing outlays as they crunch the numbers — and feel cash-poor, indebted, and decades from financial independence.

But what are you giving up then to reach that goal?

Delaying investments?

Postponing homeownership?

In the thick of struggling to make rent or bills?

If a car is putting you in cycles of debt or effectively taking away your ability to save, it's time to reconsider whether you need one at all.

OPTIONS: REDUCE FINANCIAL PRESSURE

If owning a car seems like a hassle rather than a need, here are some smarter options:

- Use Public Transport — It's not perfect, but many cities are slowly upgrading their systems — and it's much cheaper than owning a car.

- Carpooling and ride-hailing (Uber, Ola worldwide, and rare cabs for shared commutes) are popular options.

- Car ideas: Buy used or pump-saving cars. If you're in the market for a car, opting for a used model or a less expensive runabout can significantly reduce your financial burden.

- Long-Term Judging Before Purchase – When deciding on a car loan, do not judge just on the monthly EMI; check the total cost of ownership. If you can't afford it, don't.

Last Thought: A Brain Decision, not a Heart Decision

A car is a hefty financial investment, and it might not be the best choice for many young professionals. If purchasing a car requires enduring years of debt, postponing savings that could yield greater returns in the future, or experiencing constant anxiety about meeting your bills, it may be time to reconsider.

WEEKEND MOVIES: THE COSTLY HABIT OF MULTIPLEX CULTURE

The past few years have seen a major shift in entertainment, due mainly to the emergence of multiplex culture. This evolution from single-screen theaters to elaborate multiplexes has not only changed our moviegoing experience; we saw in this story last week that it has also had an outsized effect on our pocketbooks. This could be because younger people are likely to face tighter budgets and cannot afford the finances in question; however, the temptation of these contemporary movie theaters often disguises their implications when it comes to accessing the cinema and the significant amounts of money spent to do so.

Historically, going to the movies was a cheap source of entertainment — an outing that was open to many, regardless of varying income levels. Single-screen theaters provided low cost, prioritizing the film over amenities. The progress from the old days of going to a single-screen theater (at least, pre-multiplex) is visible — to a glitzy, upscale experience (at least, pre-Covid) with relatively low-ticket prices. Multiplex theaters offer upgraded technology, plush upholstery, and exclusivity — for a price. Ticket prices have reportedly increased dramatically, especially at peak weekend times and within prime time viewing windows when audiences are the most likely to come out. For example, the same movie ticket that would have cost you INR 100 in the past, now costs upwards of INR 300 in a multiplex. Although this appears to be yet another payment for an enhanced experience, frequent visitor counts pile up astronomically, both in terms of maintaining a personal bank account.

The cost of multiplex cinemas goes beyond ticket prices. Inside, there are many, many ways for patrons to spend more — money. Stands and counters around the host venues typically dispenses food and beverage products, often at inflated prices relative to the general market. A simple snack, like popcorn and a drink, could also easily double the price of going to a movie. Although purchasing snacks at the theater enhances the whole experience, it is nonetheless crucial to realize the long-term financial effects of indulging every time.

The movies once were a simple, cheap joy. All you needed was a few tickets, some popcorn, and a fun night out. But today? A night at a multiplex is now more luxurious purchase than casual entertainment.

Multiplexes have fundamentally rewired how we watch movies with plush recliners, giant screens, and surround sound that makes every action-movie explosion feel real. But with those improvements come ever-higher prices. Something that used to represent a low-cost treat for a weekend has become a money pit, especially for students and young professionals struggling to make ends meet.

WHY IS IT SO EXPENSIVE TO GO TO MOVIES NOW?

In the past, single-screen movie theaters were the norm. Tickets were inexpensive, and the emphasis was on the film itself, not on the ambience. But over time, as multiplex culture ascended, attitudes changed:

Better technology, better seating, better experience — at a price.

Weekend and prime-time ticket prices are typically 3–4 times what they used to be.

Costs are also higher with special screenings, IMAX and 3D formats.

A ticket that once used to cost INR 100 a few years back has now easily crossed INR 300-500 — and that too for a basic seat. If you're buying tickets for premium seats, you'll have to spend even more.

And that's only for the ticket price.

The Hidden Costs of Going Out to a Movie

Entering a multiplex, it's close to guaranteed that your spending will top what you had intended.

- Overpriced Snacks: If you're looking for popcorn, nachos, soft drinks, and other staples of the cinema experience, be prepared for concession stands that charge double or triple what you would pay for these same treats outside the theater. A tub of popcorn that would cost ₹50 anywhere else is easily ₹250 at a multiplex.

- Parking fees: Multiplexes are mostly located inside the malls, and hence, paid parking is almost inevitable. If your film is three hours long, add another ₹100-300 to the spending.

- SM Older but Wiser Rates: How old do I feel now that I can plop down from the front row too?

As you leave, the ₹300 movie ticket turns into a ₹1000 evening.

For students and young professionals who want to watch their wallets, that adds up quickly.

Smart Movie-Watching Tips: Balance Between Entertainment & Cost

Movies are fun, and they are a fabulous way to relax — but they shouldn't sink your finances. Here's how you can still enjoy these without spending a fortune:

- Budget for entertainment – Decide how much to spend on movies and free time each month so you won't go broke.

- Find Discounts & Offers – Most multiplexes have discounts on shows during weekdays or early morning. Some even have subscription plans that gradually reduce ticket prices.

- Avoid the Concessions or Buy in Advance — Bring your own food (where permitted) or have a meal before you catch the movie to steer clear of pricey food.

- Think about Streaming Instead – You can watch movies at home – on platforms like Netflix, Amazon Prime, and Disney+ – for a fraction of the cost. It's not a theater experience, but it's a beneficial way to save money for those who want to.

- Select Multiplexes with Free Parking—If – If you have several theaters nearby, select the one that's not charging for parking. It's a slight change, but any little bit helps.

THE BIGGER PICTURE: EXPERIENTIAL VERSUS FINANCIAL SPENDING

Movies are not just entertainment; they are a shared cultural experience. But that doesn't mean the cost is automatically worth it.

While ₹2000 per month on movies does not seem bad, over the year that is ₹24,000, which can be saved or invested or used for some future goal.

Have fun at the movies but take good care of your money. After all, entertainment should enrich your life, not diminish your financial stability.

GOING FROM SAVING TO SPENDING

This was India in the 1990s, where folks back at home did a lot of saving. Frugality was a way of life. Spending was purposeful, reserved for special occasions. Families drew pride from spending smartly and saving for the future.

It was as if I had stepped into another world when I came back in 2025." India is now an aspirational society of consumers— a spending society. Shopping malls were bustling, weddings were extravagant affairs, and credit cards were in high demand.

It put me in mind of the U.S.'s "spend now, think later" mentality.

Let's dig into what happened over the decades — how income rose and savings plummeted when spending became the focus.

Short and Savings Focused: Life in 1990

Income and Spending Habits

Income: A middle-class family earned ₹10,000–₹15,000 a month.

Saving Rate: Families saved 30–40% their income.

Expenditure: We prudently spent almost all of our money on food, clothing, and utilities. We had never eaten in restaurants or bought expensive things.

Financial Discipline

Loans were the final step, to be taken only for a house or an education.

Barely anybody had credit cards.

Families put needs above wants.

LIVING IN 2025: SHOPPING ON STEROIDS

Income and Spending Habits

Income: Middle-class families earn ₹1,00,000–₹1,50,000 a month today.

Saving Rate: Saving fell below 10 percent of income.

Spending: The costs of lifestyle — luxury items, vacations, and gadgets — occupy a large swath of budgets.

A Culture of Debt

From holidays to weddings, loans and EMIs fund big-ticket purchases.

"Interest-free" credit cards are used cavalierly, with no regard for interest or how and when debt will be repaid.

Example:

A ₹1,00,000 flagship smartphone is purchased through EMI. 12 months at 10% interest Monthly payments: ₹8,792 That is ₹5,504 more in charges — an amount that could have been saved or invested.

Comparing Then and Now: A comparison of monthly budgets in 1999 vs. 2025, highlighting the shifts in spending priorities over time:

Category	1999 (₹10,000/ month)	2025 (₹1,00,000/ month)	Observations
Basic Essentials (Food, Utilities, Schooling)	₹5,000 (50%)	₹30,000 (30%)	The cost of living has increased significantly, but as a percentage of income, it's reduced.
Savings	₹3,000 (30%)	₹10,000 (10%)	Savings rate has dropped, even with higher income.
Leisure (Dining, Entertainment)	₹1,000 (10%)	₹20,000 (20%)	Entertainment spending has increased 20x in absolute terms.

Lifestyle (Gadgets, EMIs, Travel)	₹0	₹30,000 (30%)	Previously not a major category, now a huge expense due to consumerism & debt culture.
Miscellaneous	₹1,000 (10%)	₹10,000 (10%)	Remains stable as a percentage of income but higher in absolute terms.

Key Takeaways: Basic needs now take up a smaller share of income, but their costs have risen dramatically.

♦ Lifestyle and leisure expenses have surged, driven by consumerism, tech, and travel trends.

♦ Savings have dropped from 30% to just 10%, highlighting higher spending priorities over financial security.

♦ Debt and EMIs play a huge role in 2025 budgets, whereas in 1999, people relied more on savings than loans.

Conclusion: Higher incomes in 2025 have led to greater discretionary spending but less financial security. The shift from need-based spending to lifestyle-driven expenses shows how modern financial habits are increasingly shaped by social pressure, consumer trends, and easy credit availability.

Savings dropped from 30 per cent to 10 per cent, while lifestyle and entertainment spending increased tenfold.

Weddings Then vs. Now

1999: A simple celebration at home or at a local hall cost me about ₹1–₹2 lakhs you saved over a couple of years.

2025: Destination weddings and five-star venues cost Rs 20–50 lakhs are often funded by loans

The Cost of Consumerism

Inflation and Cost of Living

Everything now costs astronomically more. What used to cost around 50 dollars in 1999 now costs around 500 dollars.

Social pressures

Social media encourages us all to spend more. Over-the-top lifestyles shared on social media feed a "fear of missing out" (FOMO) that lures many into overspending to keep up.

Example:

Riya, a 28-year-old computer engineer, took a trip to Maldives worth ₹3 lakhs by using a personal loan. Her two-year annual ₹15,000 monthly EMI did not give her a margin to save or invest.

Lessons from the Past

Save First: Reserve 20–30% of your income before any spending happens.

Skip Debt You Don't Need: Consider before borrowing — is it a need or a want?

Be frugal: Save for the long-run, not for the short-run

In closing: Spend Wisely, Save Wisest

It was a shift from saving to spending — a change that brought improved living standards but also financial risks. Higher incomes don't mean much when expenses expand even more quickly.

To escape the cycle of debt, we need to adopt the values of our parents' generation — save for tomorrow; live within our means; spend with intention. Only then can we afford financial freedom with all the wonderful things in life.

FINAL THOUGHTS

Has your lifestyle changed in ways that negatively affect your net worth (debt or savings)? This chapter explores your relationship with how your lifestyle, especially in eating out, is harming your finances. Many people succumb to the allure of instant gratification and peer pressure, leading them to habitually dine out without realizing the cumulative costs. These costs are not limited to the monetary budget; the absence of healthy food is provided by numerous sources, but nonetheless, you can get sick from too much junk food, and often higher medical costs are incurred. Personalizing at a granular level enables people to see how they might approach their eating patterns in alignment with greater financial priorities.

Solar Plexus: By integrating social and financial constraints in a collaborative manner, whether it's through visible actions such as reducing social outings, or less obvious ones such as dedicating more time to researching healthier and cost-effective meal preparation or imposing limits on regular activities that drain your social funds, you can reframe your approach and maximize your enjoyment of life without negatively impacting your monthly finances.

With these takeaways in mind, young adults and college students should take the time to assess spending decisions through the perspective of their long-term goals. Embracing strategies that promote financial independence and align with your values is a significant benefit of this newfound independence. Constraining spending, implementing tools to keep budgeting up to date, and finding purposeful substitutes for movement and social excursions allow for the formation of financially sustainable habits without compromising on richer experiences. This tactic not only gets them one step closer to finding a more financially healthy future, but it also leads them to make healthier lifestyle choices along the way.

Chapter 6

STRATEGIES FOR PERSONAL FINANCIAL MANAGEMENT

Proper management of personal finances is an important foundation for independence and an essential feature, which every adult should possess, regardless of where he is in the world. In the universe of often life-changing and always long-lasting financial decisions, positioning yourself to better understand how to negotiate options is essential. If you're a college student enjoying financial independence for the first time or a new graduate grappling with the realities of balancing income with debt, you need a plan that works. When young adults in India embark on their financial trajectory, a few soft skills can contribute to an enlightening outcome. "Nonetheless, it is not only better to be cautious about money matters, but also to make efforts to improve it and grow."

In this chapter, you will learn several strategies that are here to provide you with the tools that you need to better manage your money in personal finance. Exploring methods for managing costs, establishing budgets that make financial sense, and setting realistic targets are some of the topics readers will discover that are essential for achieving financial stability in these pages. The text manual will provide advice on how to prioritize bills and also how actions and plans should change as things do in your life to make your plans relevant. Additionally, the focus will be more on developing positive payment habits and creative ways to pay off debt. Written as if you were sitting across from you in a coffee shop having a discussion on practical advice for your life; this chapter is designed to be practical, offering a clear roadmap for those who want to become better financial thinkers in the real world and take control of their financial future.

A GUIDE TO FINANCIAL ROAD-MAPPING YOUR PATH

Money is personal. It informs our decisions, our autonomy, and our future. But for many young adults — whether you're a college student, for the first time learning how to manage money, or a recent graduate trying to balance income and debt — navigating finances can feel overwhelming.

The fact is that money is more than numbers. It's about your habits, decisions, and knowledge of how to leverage your income. As young professionals in India take control of their financial future, a few essential skills can significantly impact their success. It's not only about being frugal about how to invest it; multiply it and let it serve you.

WHAT YOU'LL LEARN IN THIS CHAPTER

This chapter, which is more than just a collection of financial tips, is a conversation, the kind you'd have over coffee with a friend who's been there. You'll explore:

- This article explains how to create a budget that is effective in real life, not just one that looks appealing on paper.

- Savvy strategies to keep costs down so you don't end up scrambling at the month's end.

- Actual ways to manage debt — be it student loans, credit cards or surprise bills.

- How to prioritize where you spend your money, without sounding like you're always saying "no" to a good time.

- What works today may not work tomorrow, so financial plans should accommodate life changes.

A REAL-WORLD APPROACH

Good money management is hardly about perfection. It's about progress. A successful financial plan evolves as your life evolves — just like changing your morning coffee order when you discover that the third shot of espresso isn't worth the jitters.

In this chapter, you'll find practical, field-tested advice. Consider this less a lecture than a financial toolkit. The goal? The goal is to assist you in gaining greater control over your finances, enabling you to make decisions that align with your desired life.

Because personal finance, at its core, is not about restriction, it's about freedom.

DEBT MANAGEMENT TECHNIQUES

Understanding Debt: What You Owe and How to Tackle It

Debt can seem like a burden you're always carrying — sometimes manageable, sometimes overwhelming. However, not all debt is created equal, and knowing the different types of debt can help you pay off smarter.

The Two Main Types of Debt

Because at the center of debt, there are two types:

Secured Debt – This type of debt is backed by collateral, so there's something tangible on the line. Think about home loans (mortgages) or car loans — if you don't pay up, the lender can reclaim the asset.

Unsecured Debt – This means there's no physical asset tied to the loan, which is why these tend to come with higher interest rates. These include credit cards, personal loans, and student loans.

Why does this matter? Because when it comes to choosing which debts to pay first, it's helpful to emphasize the ones that could end up costing you the most, whether that means losing your house or accruing interest charges that soar into the stratosphere.

HOW TO BREAK THE DEBT CYCLE: PROVEN STRATEGIES

After you've lined up all your debts, the next step can seem daunting. Where do you even start? That's where a systematized plan comes into play.

Debt Snowball: For The Win, The Big Win

A Simple but Effective Approach:

List all your debts in ascending order, disregarding the interest rates for the time being.

Make minimum payments on everything but the smallest debt — use any extra cash to eliminate it.

Once the smallest debt is paid off, move to the next one — and so forth.

It's all about momentum. You can pay off a small debt quickly, which gives you a quick win, boosting confidence and keeping you motivated. It's kind of like exercise — you know it's good for you, but once you start seeing some results, you want to keep going.

- ♦ Case study: A recent college graduate overwhelmed by student debt began implementing this strategy. He started by clearing a small balance on his credit card, which gave him the momentum to tackle his next debt — and before he knew it, he'd eliminated half his liabilities in a matter of months.

DEALING WITH CREDITORS: YES, YOU CAN

Here's something a lot of people don't presumably realize: Lenders would rather work with you than receive nothing at all. If you're having trouble, simply picking up the phone and asking for better terms may be to your benefit.

What to ask for?

- ♦ A lower interest rate
- ♦ Reduced monthly payments

♦ An extended repayment plan

◊ Real-life example: A recent college graduate, burdened with education loans, approached his lender and successfully negotiated a reduced interest rate, which provided him with much-needed financial relief.

It may feel daunting, but they can only say no. And if they say yes? That's cash in your pocket.

Building an emergency fund: Your safety net

If debt is a hole, an emergency fund is the safety rope that prevents you from falling deeper in." Life presents surprises — a medical bill, a car repair, a loss of income — and without a buffer, those costs invariably add more debt.

How to Get Started (Even If You're Broke)

Start small — even ₹500 or ₹1,000 a month compounds.

Put surprise cash to good use — bonuses, tax refunds or gifts can give a boost to your fund.

Automate savings — establish a transfer to a separate account so you don't even have to think about it.

♦ Tip in Action: After a recent graduate landed her first job, she simply began rounding up odd change at the end of every week. In a year, he had saved enough to weather an unexpected job loss without missing rent.

An emergency fund not only shields you financially; it lowers your stress levels, which makes you less likely to panic-spend or take out high-interest loans when something goes awry.

HOW TO MAKE YOUR DEBT PLAN WORK FOR YOU

There is no universal strategy for managing debt.

What is working today may require some adjustments tomorrow. That's why it's important too:

- ◆ Monitor your progress – Celebrate small victories to stay motivated.

- ◆ Reevaluate if necessary — If your income varies, adjust your plan.

- ◆ Stay flexible — Your financial life will change, and your repayment plan should too.

Debt is more than just numbers — it's about control. The objective isn't merely ridding yourself of what you owe; it's obtaining financial liberation for the ability to concentrate on what genuinely counts in life.

BUDGET CREATION FUNDAMENTALS

Budgets 101: A Hands-On Guide to Taking Charge of Your Money

In all honesty, budgeting is not a particularly enjoyable task. But if you want financial independence, it's a skill you can't avoid. The good news? Budgets aren't a limitation — they're a controlling mechanism. It's crucial to make your money work for you, not the other way around.

STEP 1: KNOW WHERE YOUR MONEY COMES FROM.

You need to know how much money is coming in before deciding.

Income for many young adults in India may come from a variety of sources:

A part-time job or internship

Scholarships or a parental allowance

Freelancing or side hustles

Your first full-time post-college gig

If you're making money in multiple ways, be meticulous tracking it — you don't want to undervalue how much you'll bring in and find yourself running out of cash before the month ends.

STEP 2: FIND OUT WHERE YOUR MONEY GOES.

This is where it gets real. Ever think to yourself, where does my paycheck go? By tracking your expenses, you can see where your money is going.

A good place to start is by categorizing expenses:

- Necessities – Things like rent, food, transportation, utilities
- Lifestyle — Streaming services, dining out, shopping
- Savings & Investments -- Emergency fund, retirement, debt payments

Here's a familiar shock: a lot of people pay much more for meals or subscriptions than they think they do. Maybe those daily runs for coffee or multiple streaming accounts are more expensive than you realized. The fact that you can see so clearly what you're spending makes it easier to adjust your habits without feeling deprived.

STEP 3: MAKE REALISTIC GOALS (IMMEDIATE & FUTURE)

Budgeting is most effective when you have specific goals. These could be:

Immediate goals – Building savings for a new laptop, a vacation or even an emergency fund

Long-term goals—Paying off student loans, investing, or purchasing a vehicle

The key is to set realistic goals. If you set impossible goals (like saving half your paycheck when you can barely pay rent), you'll only wind up disheartened. Begin with modest successes — even putting away ₹500 to ₹1,000 a month matters in the long term.

STEP 4: REVIEW & ADAPT AS LIFE CHANGES

Your budget is subject to change. Life happens. You could receive a raise, relocate to a new city, or incur surprise expenses. That's why it's important to check in frequently.

Did your rent increase? Adjust.

Are you earning more? Maybe increase your savings.

Did you spend more than expected last month? See where you can cut back.

Flexibility in your budget lets you take the reins without frustration.

STEP 5: BUDGETING IS A TOOL, NOT A CONSTRAINT

So many people think of budgeting as restrictive, but it's liberating. Why? It helps to alleviate stress. When you have your money broken down into how much is available for what, you can prevent running out and experiencing guilt spending on things you enjoy.

For instance, you may prioritize traveling over purchasing the latest gadgets. Once you've disclosed your spending, adjust your budget to reflect your values without guilt.

STEP 6: USE TECHNOLOGY TO YOUR ADVANTAGE

Budgeting isn't always manual or boring. There are plenty of budgeting apps that can track transactions, categorize spending, and remind you about bills. Setting up automated savings can also simplify life — arrange for a small transfer to your savings account every payday so you're steadily building a safety net.

STEP 7: KEEP TRACK OF SAVINGS & DEBT MANAGEMENT

If you have student loans or other debt, budgeting helps you make repayments stress-free. A simple trick? Put aside a set amount each month for debt payments — just as you would for rent or groceries — so it doesn't seem so intimidating.

And what about emergency funds — life happens. An unexpected medical bill or car repair can decline your finances if you're not ready. And even if you can save only ₹1,000 a month, it is something. In the long run, this fund saves you from loans or credit cards in dire situations.

Final Thoughts: Your Budget = Your Freedom

Budgeting isn't a way to say no to everything — it's a way to say yes to what really matters. A well-thought-out budget allows you to:

- Open Wallet to Provide Essentials

- Save for things you really want

- Steps to prevent falling into debt traps and anxiety

And most importantly, it is your money in your control and not the other way around.

UNDERSTANDING INCOME AND EXPENSE FLOWS

What You Need to Know About Income and Expenses

Money comes in, money goes out — but do you really know where it all goes? If you've ever wondered why your paycheck seems to vanish so quickly, you're not alone. Cash flow — the flow of money in and out of your life — is an important financial skill. It's the basis of making wise decisions, preventing financial anxiety, and creating a solid future.

Your income is literally the lifeblood of your organization.

Most people think of income simply as their salary. But closer inspection may reveal that you have more income streams than you thought.

A job (whether full- or part-time)

Do freelance work or side hustles

Scholarships, grants or stipends

Family support (some money from mum and dad or relatives)

Small business earnings.

Viewing income holistically will help you consider all your options and inspire you to find new sources.

STEP 1: FOLLOW YOUR EXPENSES

Spending money is easy. Tracking it? I don't think so. But knowing where your money goes is the secret to spending with intent rather than mindlessly.

One of the best places to start is to divide your expenses between fixed costs and variable costs:

- Required or fixed costs: rent, utilities, loan payments, transportation

- Expenses that fluctuate: Groceries, dining, shopping, and entertainment

Ever your bank state of mind statement and thought, "wait, what?" Perhaps your daily coffee habits or streaming subscriptions are costing you more than you thought. Small leaks like these can gnaw at your finances over time. (If eating out is making your budget teeter, say swapping a couple restaurant meals for home-cooked ones could save you thousands over a year without "feeling like a total sacrifice," as Hetherington puts it.)

STEP 2: SURPLUS OR DEFICIT?

When you've lined up your income and expenses, it's time for the big question: Do you end the month with extra cash or run low?

Surplus? Great! You can use that additional money for savings, investments, or to reduce debt quickly.

Deficit? Now is the time to make some changes — either by reducing needless spending or finding ways to make extra money.

Regularly checking your cash flow (at least monthly) allows you to stay in control. Becoming unprepared for a financial shortfall when rent is due is the worst scenario.

STEP 3: RECALIBRATE YOU'RE PLANNING WISELY

Once you know where your money is going, you can begin making small yet effective changes.

Car or public transport? Fuel, insurance, and maintenance costs all reinforce that owning a vehicle could potentially be very expensive. If public transport is a practical option, it might save you thousands of dollars every year.

Are we talking about expensive outings and free activities? Slashing expensive entertainment doesn't mean killing all the joy — you just need to use that imagination. Cheap parks, local events, and home movie nights can be just as fun as an expensive night out.

Impulse shopping or intentional spending? If you're someone who buys things on a whim, implement a 24-hour rule — wait for a day on any nonessential purchase. If you still want it after 24 hours, it's probably worth it.

Changes like that add up and make a big difference in your financial security over time.

STEP 4: TACKLE HIGH-INTEREST DEBT FIRST

Debt — especially high-interest debt — can be a silent financial killer. The longer it hangs around, the closer courtesy comes to compound interest.

If you have leftover money at the end of each month, high on your list should be debt repayments (especially credit cards or personal loans). Once you've paid off your debt, you'll have more money to invest, save, or allocate towards more significant financial goals.

STEP 5: CONTINUE CHECK-INS AND ADJUSTING

Life isn't static. Your income could rise, your expenses could change, and your financial goals could evolve. That's why reviewing your budget and cash flow regularly is critical.

Got a raise? Save a higher percentage of your income.

Moved to a new city? Reassess your budget.

Unexpected expense? Revise your financial plan to suffer the blow.

This is critical for young adults entering the labor market. While your initial salary may seem insignificant, as your income increases, so should your financial plan.

Final Thought: Control Your Money, Don't Let It Control You

Ultimately, money should serve as a tool to help you shape the life you desire, not a cause of worry. With a clear picture of your income, where your money is going, and some small, smart tweaks, you can create financial balance (although there may be small sacrifices along the way) and lay the foundation for success (even if it takes time).

SETTING FINANCIAL GOALS: A PRACTICAL APPROACH TO BUILDING WEALTH

The systematic technique to wealth building — Setting Financial Goals

Money without a plan is like driving without a map—you can get somewhere but probably not where you wanted to go. No matter how new you are in your financial journey or how much work you have left to do, establishing clear, attainable goals has the power to help you make progress and stay motivated — giving you ownership over your future.

Start Small: The Power of Short-Term Goals

Many financial goals — like buying a home or retiring on comfortable terms — can seem daunting. Therefore, it's crucial to set short-term goals.

Therefore, it's crucial to set short-term goals.

They generate confidence, hold you accountable, and make financial discipline feel rewarding instead of withholding.

Short-term—you want to accomplish something in one year. Some examples include:

- Investing ₹10,000 in an emergency fund

- Reducing a small debt (e.g. a credit line)

- Saving up on a new laptop, a vacation, or training course

The key is to break it down into smaller segments. Say you want to save ₹10,000 in six months; that's roughly ₹1,700 a month or ₹55 a day. Suddenly, it feels doable. Arranging for automatic transfers to a savings account can make it seamless, so you don't need to depend on willpower.

As money management is truly a muscle, each small victory adds to your momentum and bigger victories financially in the future!

Thinking Big: Long-Term Financial Planning

Instant gratifications are nice, but true financial freedom is the product of foresight. Long-term goals are generally five years or more and can include:

- Buying a home

- Starting a business

- Planning for retirement

- Investing in future wealth

You need a different mindset for long-term goals. You can't simply trim expenses or save pennies; It takes real leverage, like investing, career advancement or passive income streams, to generate wealth over time.

Staying flexible is also key. Life changes — jobs, relationships, the economy — so reviewing and recalibrating your goals every few months makes sure they remain relevant. Long-term financial success is all about consistency, not perfection."

Tracking Progress: Staying Accountable

Setting goals is easy. Sticking to them? That's the challenging part. That's why you must track your progress periodically.

Once a month, check in on your finances — find out what's working and what you need to change.

Monitor your spending and saving habits with budgeting apps or basic spreadsheets.

It will show you the pros and cons of comparing your savings percentage to your income.

Example: A 20-something set a short-term savings goal: to save 20% of their monthly income. After keeping a record of their expenses, they discovered that they were spending too much on eating out and paid services. A few small adjustments — like eating at home more and canceling an unused membership — got them to their goal without deprivation.

The goal is not perfection — it's awareness. Regular check-ins will reduce financial surprises and keep you more in control of your money.

Make It Personal: Goals That Actually Motivate You

Money goals aren't all about the numbers. Writing them according to your values and priorities makes them more meaningful and easier to keep.

If travel makes your heart sing, instead of splurging on luxury items, you can decide to save ₹50,000 a year for travel instead.

If education is a priority, you might save time to take classes or continue your education to build your career.

If sustainability is a consideration, you may opt to invest in companies that promote it or funds that focus on renewable energy.

When your financial goals align with what you care about, staying disciplined doesn't feel like a sacrifice; it's just a choice.

Final Thought: Small Steps, Big Impact

It takes time to build financial stability — that doesn't happen overnight. It's about doing the right thing — consistently — setting smaller, achievable goals, measuring progress, and adapting along the way.

Lesson: It's less about your income and more about your management. Begin small, think long-term, and stay flexible. Each step you take reinforces the financial independence you desire.

REVIEWING AND ADJUSTING FINANCIAL PLANS

Keep It on Track: Review and Re-assess Your Financial Plan

Money isn't static. Life happens, expenses change, and financial goals change. This is why it's crucial to regularly update your financial plan. It's so much like a health check-up for your money. Taking a moment to reassess is a chance to catch bad habits, identify new opportunities, and ensure your plan still aligns with your present reality.

STEP 1: DO A THOROUGH ANALYSIS OF YOUR SPENDING.

Where does your money really go each month? You may think you know, but small expenses can really add up—quickly.

Ride-sharing services. Those spontaneous journeys could potentially cost thousands of dollars annually.

Subscription services? Do you really need four streaming services?

Dining out? Even a few meals out per week could add up to more than an entire month's groceries.

A monthly "touch base" can expose things you are spending too much on. A budgeting app, or even a simple spreadsheet, can make tracking easy. It's not about eliminating everything fun — it's about understanding where your money is going and what is truly worth it."

STEP 2: EXPAND FOR CHANGED LIFE

Life happens. "Your financial plan should change depending on if you change jobs, move to another city, have an emergency expense," he says.

Got a raise? Great! Put the extra income to work before lifestyle inflation magnifies it.

New expenses? Reworking your budget can help you absorb the impact of unexpected medical bills or car repairs without delaying your long-term goals.

Big milestones ahead? Perhaps you were saving up to travel, but buying a home now seems more pressing. That's fine — all these goals change, and you should budget with that in mind.

The key is flexibility. A financial plan should serve as a guide, evolving and adapting as you do.

What you need to know before buying a house:

STEP 3: KNOW WHEN TO GET PROFESSIONAL ADVICE

A simple Google search won't yield every answer. Getting professional financial advice can sometimes save you time, money, and stress.

Confused about taxes? A tax advisor can help you maximize deductions and minimize what you own.

Drowning in student loans? The financial expert can help guide you through repayment options.

Unsure about investing? A financial planner can help you create a portfolio that makes sense according to your goals.

You don't have to be wealthy to want financial advice. Even getting advice just once is still better than doing it yourself, and that can get you thinking right and making better decisions.

STEP 4: BE FINANCIALLY FLEXIBLE

Having a plan is great. Better yet, adaptability.

Suppose your original goal was saving to travel, but now you're thinking about applying that money to a down payment on a home. That isn't failure — it's growth.

Adapting your plan to changing priorities is a sign of financial maturity, not a setback.

And what if you take a financial hit? Stay calm. A flexible financial plan helps you pivot, tighten your belt where necessary, and stay on track without feeling that you've failed."

STEP 5: MAKE FINANCIAL CHECK-INS HABITUAL

How to keep your money under your control? Make sure to check your financial plan often.

Monthly: Account for your spending, savings and any unexpected expenses.

Quarterly: Check in on progress toward larger goals — paying off debt, growing investments.

Annually: Take a deep dive — account for major life changes, assess investment performance, and establish new financial goals for the next year.

And a planned approach helps ensure you stay on track and avoid financial surprises.

STEP 6: NEVER STOP LEARNING

The world of finance is constantly evolving. Keeping up to date can create opportunities for new investment styles, help you save more efficiently, and help create better trends in your financial life.

Read books or articles about personal finance.

Study investing or money management through an online course.

Associated with finance specialists, or follow-money podcasts, podcasts based on finance, it will grow your money knowledge and make your forceful.

Knowledge is power. The more you know, the better choices you'll make.

STEP 7: TAKE THE STRESS OUT BY AUTOMATING

Let's get real—keeping track of bills, savings, and investments is no simple task. Automation makes it easier.

Automate your savings and investments so you are always accumulating wealth even if you forget.

Set up auto-pay for bills to avoid late fees and maintain a healthy credit score.

The less you need to think about these jobs, the more automatically you'll do them.

Final Thought: Keep It Simple, Stay Flexible

Financial planning is not about perfection. It's about progress. Reviewing, tweaking, and being willing to change course can keep you financially afloat, regardless of what you face." Stop allowing your money to control you; instead, have it work for you."

WHAT WE'VE LEARNED

Personal Finance: Budgeting, Debt Control and Stability

What's at stake in money management is not merely the numbers but also decisions, habits, and long-term prosperity. Chapter 7— Money Management: Budgets, Debt, and Financial Resilience. This chapter discusses how to improve personal finance, including budgeting, debt repayment, and understanding the importance of being financially resilient.

What You Owe and How to Tackle It: Understanding Debt

Not all debt is the same. Some loans give you something to lose — a home loan or a car loan, for example. Default on a few payments, and the lender can reclaim the asset. These are known as secured debts. But unsecured debts — such as credit cards or personal loans — aren't backed by collateral, which is why they tend to carry higher interest rates.

How To Prioritize Your Debt Repayment One strategy is the Debt Snowball Method, which involves paying small debts first to gain momentum and then addressing larger debts. It's not always just a matter of math; occasionally, those initial successes serve as motivation and sustain your progress.

Another key strategy? Engaging in negotiations with creditors is another crucial strategy.

Most lenders would prefer to work with you than risk getting nothing at all. Engaging in a conversation can result in significant savings over time, including the reduction of interest rates, the extension of repayment terms, and the reduction of penalties.

The Case for An Emergency Fund as Your Safety Net

Surprise expenses happen — a medical emergency, losing a job, even a last-minute flight for family issues. Without a buffer, such moments can derail your finances, leaving you to lean on high-interest loans or credit cards.]

How to build an emergency fund? Start small. Just setting aside ₹500 or ₹1,000 a month will add up over time. You want three to six months' worth of essential expenses saved ideally — but don't worry if you're not there yet. The key is consistency.

What Is Budgeting: How to Get on Top of Your Finances

A budget is about knowing where your money goes and choosing wisely, not eliminating things.

Setting a budget isn't so much about eliminating something as it is about knowing where

Here's an easy overview to help you begin:

Track your income. How much do you make? This is the revenue part of the budget: List all your sources — salary, freelance work, stipends, family support, anything bringing in money.

Categorize your expenses. Differentiate between your fixed costs (rent, utilities, loan payments) and your variable expenses (groceries, entertainment, dining out).

Set financial goals. Saving for a trip? Paying off a loan? This is where budgeting comes into play.

Use tech to your advantage. Budgeting apps or just a simple spreadsheet will make tracking that much easier and quicker.

Budgeting is critical for young professionals and students. It makes sure that an unexpected expense — for example, a laptop repair or doctor's bill — doesn't drive you into needless debt.

Making Finances Work for You

Financial stability doesn't have to look perfect. It's about making informed decisions, adapting as life transforms around you, and continuing to work toward your goals.

This chapter serves not only as a cheat sheet but also as a roadmap for young adult Indians in their journey towards financial independence. Whether you're tackling debt, setting up savings, or simply trying to increase your income, the shared goal is to develop habits that will equip you for long-term success.

Chapter 7

DEVELOPING FINANCIAL DISCIPLINE

Mastering financial discipline is key to making sound financial choices that promote long-term stability. You are limited to available information until October 2023. Conversations about money can be difficult, requiring active listening and assertiveness to handle appropriately. For young adults and recent graduates, these conversations aid them in traversing unfamiliar financial waters. They provide guidance on setting budgets, negotiating costs, and initiating conversations about common financial goals, paving the way for a solid financial base.

In this chapter, discuss the components important to developing discipline in financial decision-making. You will learn how communication skills, such as active listening, establish trust in financial conversations and how they help avoid misunderstandings. We also discuss how empathy improves financial interactions by recognizing others' situations, thus enabling collaborative problem-solving. It also dissects negotiation skills, breaking down their importance in getting fair and beneficial arrangements in everyday money matters. In this chapter, we have the objective of making sure that readers acquire a practical set of tools to maintain financial discipline during various influences and pressures.

INTERPERSONAL SKILLS FOR FINANCIAL CONVERSATIONS

Thus, developing strong communication skills is essential for managing finances, especially for young adults and recent graduates beginning their journey into the economic world. Honing these skills can have a profound effect on how people face challenging situations with money, as well as make financially literate decisions when it matters most. Active listening is one of the most important aspects because it cultivates the trust and understanding of both parties in monetary matters. Listening to others' financial insights and values helps you find better messages and sell more. For example, if you are talking to a partner or roommate about budgeting, actively listening to their concerns and priorities can help create an atmosphere where one side is not trying to "one-up" the other's needs (Great Expectations).

In addition to listening, assertiveness in financial conversations is also crucial. With assertiveness, people can confidently express their financial needs or limitations. Such skill brings clarity and keeps financial strain due to miscommunication at bay. Imagine a young adult trying to negotiate a raise at work; being assertive helps them to communicate their value effectively within the organization. Also, this confidence is vital when establishing limits on monetary contributions. Learning to say no to expenses that don't win in the long run is an act of financial self-preservation and accountability.

Empathy in conversations about money, built upon assertiveness, can guide a compassionate response to shared financial challenges. Expressing empathy includes understanding and considering an emotional component of financial matters, which often results in better relationships and a more collaborative approach to resolving others' problems. For instance, within a college student splitting rent with roommates, someone could show empathy by recognizing different financial means and collaboratively coming to a mutually fair agreement. This helps reduce tension between the parties involved and builds goodwill and mutual aid among them.

One of the keys to exchanging finance is building negotiation skills. These skills help people negotiate for mutually beneficial deals and resolve conflicts about money. Effective negotiation involves preparation, knowledge of the interests of all parties involved, and the ability to formulate imaginative solutions that please everyone. Consider a situation in which newly graduated students are planning to travel together. With the use of negotiation skills, they can come together and designate a budget and a plan that suits different people's financial means and still provide a great experience for everyone."

From a practical perspective, being able to negotiate is immensely useful when it comes to work — whether that be negotiating salaries or benefits packages. The ability to negotiate is a valuable skill that can be applied in many areas of life, helping people get the terms they deserve desensitized by the value of kinds or amounts of things, essentially what is within a handful. This ability to arrive at equitable compromises leads to better financial results as time goes on.

From Soil to Stall: How Farms and Dining Have Changed

In the 1990s, most families in India, especially village families, grew their own food. Farming was never solely a business; it was a lifestyle. Families tended gardens and animals and ate what they produced. Now fast-forward to 2025: everything looks quite different. The younger generations are entirely divorced from farming in cities. They rely on the market for simple vegetables and usually pay a high price for them.

In this chapter, we delve into the shift from self-reliance to reliance on the market, the evolution of our appetites, and the monetary costs associated with the convenience of purchasing food from stores.

OUR LIFE ON THE FARM DURING MY FATHER'S TIME

Most rural households in my father's time owned small segments of land, which they used to cultivate their own food. Here's how they managed:

A Self-Sufficient Life

They farmed staples like rice, wheat, and lentils.

From their gardens came vegetables like tomatoes, okra, brinjal, and spinach.

Livestock provided milk and eggs and sometimes meat.

Minimal Trips to the Market

Most of their food needs come from home.

Any surplus produce was sold or bartered locally, establishing a small but steady income stream.

Low Costs

Seeds and manure were either home-produced or locally sourced.

Grocery prices, on the other hand, were far cheaper than we see now.

The Shift in 2025

This self-sufficient lifestyle has all but disappeared in cities today and in some rural areas.

Dependence on markets

They now buy the majority, if not all, of their food.

Even vegetables and fruits have no longer come from our gardens but have been purchased in supermarkets or online stores.

Rising Costs

Inflation has raised the cost of basic staples dramatically.

So, if you spent ₹10 on vegetables in the 1990s, it could be ₹100 or more today.

Loss of Skills

They don't know how to grow their own food.

From generation to generation, families used to pass down the art of farming and tilling the land; young people now forget how to do this.

THE COST OF MARKET DEPENDENCY

Let's do the math on the financial difference:

Example: Monthly Grocery Cost (1990 to 2025)

1990: A family of four spent ₹500–₹1,000 on food per month. The bulk of it was for things they could not grow, like salt, oil, and spices.

2025: This family now spends ₹8,000–₹10,000 a month just on groceries, the essentials such as vegetables and fruits.

Scenario: A Bag of Tomatoes

1990: One kilo tomato: ₹2–₹5 Most families grew their own, so there were few opportunities for market purchases.

2025: The same kilo is ₹50–₹100 now, depending on the season and the city.

The Bigger Picture

Shifting from growing food to buying it has resulted in:

Soaring Costs: Families spend a sizable part of their income on groceries these days.

Less control: people depend on market prices and supply chains.

Commercial agriculture uses chemicals more than traditional farming, which has a significant negative impact on nature services.

A Personal Reflection

Looking back at my father's era, life was so much easier and cheaper. Families grew their own food with pride. More than one middle-aged person pointed out that before it became most people's sad and dreary (and expensive) primary source of nourishment, they were eating fresh, healthy meals sans the worries of inflated prices or pesticide residue.

Today, convenience has replaced that. It is easier to buy food, but that has a financial and environmental price.

Lessons We Can Learn

Grow What You Can: Even if you have a small garden at home, growing your own food can reduce expenses and provide fresh produce.

Support Local Farmers: You're helping small farmers when you buy from them directly. You'll get fresher, less expensive produce.

Minimize Waste: Consider doing some meal planning and only purchase what you need to minimize food and money waste.

CONCLUSION: FINDING A BALANCE

Modern conveniences have done much to improve livability while distancing us from baseline self-sufficiency. Together, with the best of the past and the tools we have today, we can build a tomorrow where we spend smarter, eat healthier, and live more sustainably.

HANDLING SOCIETY EXPECTATIONS

To reach financial independence, we have to understand the impact society has on spending decisions. For the youth of India — college students just starting a financial journey and young graduates navigating the job market — society is a huge influence on financial decisions, most often subconsciously.

The first step when beginning to identify progressive, winning norms is to identify societal norms. The unwritten rules that groups in a community follow are known as societal norms. This is because, for example, these norms typically inform our definitions of success, consumption, and lifestyle, all of which tend to establish standards that many feel pressured to achieve. Consumer goods, brands, and waiter dinner experiences are just a few examples of the ubiquitous presence of these norms today.

Comprehending these norms empowers individuals to discern the standards they adhere to and the ones that could potentially lead them astray. This type of awareness is empowering — returning control to the person and allowing them to make more informed decisions about what matters most to them financially.

When you are aware of these norms, the next step is to establish individual boundaries. This can lead people to put more importance in "keeping up with the Jones'" over and abandoning their priorities. Setting clear boundaries is crucial to exercising self-discipline against external social pressure. That involves making a choice about where your money goes and then fighting the urge to buy more than you are responsible for living up to external standards. One crucial guideline for achieving this is to implement a budgeting system, which involves setting aside specific amounts for necessities, savings, and discretionary spending and ensuring adherence to it. By doing this, you not only prevent debt but also establish the foundation for long-term financial stability.

Just as crucial, however, is articulating these boundaries. It's one thing to internally set limits, but sharing that with others — friends, family, or co-workers — instills respect for your financial decisions. It can be as simple as saying, "I'm trying to save at the moment," when you are invited to a pricey outing. Establishing this upfront sets the standard and has the potential to relieve the strain of needing to meet someone else's financial standards. Saying "No" can be daunting, but by consistently communicating your financial boundaries, you solidify them for both you and the people around you, creating respect and understanding.

Embracing Individual Values: Another Pillar of Financial DisciplineWhen it comes to practicing financial discipline amidst mounting societal pressures, embracing individual values is another pillar. And, in a world always trying to dictate who we "should" be and what we "should" own, knowing what is important to us is a compass. Practicing values-based investing: Values-based investing means making fiscal decisions that reflect your values and priorities, not the latest trends. Let's say travel makes you feel real happiness and aligns with your value of exploration and learning. Those who follow this philosophy should save for experiences rather than be influenced by the latest gadget if it doesn't matter to them.

To focus on individual values sometimes means standing apart from the crowd, something that does require courage. But it is this distinction that causes you to feel fulfilled while also gaining wealth/free time. This is not always a simple process, especially in cultures where there is a focus on collective identity, but it liberates individuals to follow what they actually want to do, both financially and otherwise.

ACTIVE LISTENING IN FINANCIAL DISCOURSE

Young adults and graduates taking the first steps in their financial life need to develop financial discipline. A frequently underappreciated — but crucial — skill toward this end is active listening. If the true basis of financial matters discussions is listening, then it is by extension a real-life practice of learning to understand other perspectives and setting the stage for discussions.

When confidential matters arise, it is difficult to trust each other without true engagement during financial discussions. Arguably, the best way to honor the hearts and minds of others is through presence. [Read: How to Handle Holiday Debt]. This validation establishes a foundation for connection and can facilitate the discussion of challenging topics like budgeting or debt repayment. For instance, in a conversation about how someone splits expenses with a roommate or partner, displays of attention to the speaker and empathy can transform misunderstandings into mutual understanding and a common sense of respect.

It pays to appreciate the other person's perspective to make sound financial decisions. Purposeful listening creates understanding of the complexities of other viewpoints, leading to changed behavior. Take, for example, a recent graduate exploring a friend's business venture. By actively listening to the friend's vision and concerns, the graduate proactively draws on this information to facilitate informed decision-making based on risk and opportunity. These viewpoints guarantee that decisions don't occur in isolation but rather reflect a diverse range of ideas and experiences.

By framing listening as a foundational ability, you set a tone of understanding within which the conversations you need to have around finances can evolve. Rooms can become tense, with participants caught between clashing priorities and emotional pressure. However, when all parties experience a sense of being heard and understood, it facilitates a more collaborative approach to navigating these complexities. Consider the scenario of a college student struggling to arrange a family vacation within a tight budget. He listens carefully, and the student devises solutions. The process promotes cooperation instead of agitation and demands that any agreements reached reflect the interests and constraints of all the parties involved.

Listening also helps the counselor identify deep-rooted financial beliefs and behaviors that may be skewed. Many of us have unarticulated beliefs about money that we learned from our upbringing or personal experiences. Through attentive listening, we can uncover these implicit attitudes. For instance, a recent graduate may realize through active listening that their partner has mixed feelings about saving, possibly due to a past with financial insecurity. Then they can get to the core reason for it, not just to outside behavior. The new knowledge brings about an actual transformation of the shared management of wealth.

The first step to practicing active listening with your finances is mindfulness. Get rid of distractions, be attentive to the speaker, and concentrate. Repeat and rephrase the main ideas back to them for clarity and to indicate your listening. Also, ask open-ended questions that push a little deeper." That not only clarifies what is understood but demonstrates that you are genuinely interested in what they are thinking and feeling."

Reflective listening is an additional tool that involves repeating or paraphrasing the speaker's words to verify your understanding. Reflective listening ensures accurate understanding and allows the speaker to delve deeper into the discussion. So, if someone says they're worried about a financial decision, reply: "It sounds like you're concerned about what this investment might mean for your future. Can you speak more about that?'" This encourages further discussion and shows your willingness to work together on the bill.

HOW TO NEGOTIATE: A 3-STEP PROCESS THAT CAN SAVE YOU MONEY & BUILD RELATIONSHIPS

Discussing finances can lead to unpleasant Rent division between roommates, vacation costs with a partner, and negotiating a raise at work are just a few examples of financial chats that come with tension. That's negotiation—not of a battle, but of a tool to find common ground, mitigate conflicts, and find fair results.

For many people, negotiation seems like something that happens in corporate boardrooms or high-stakes business deals. Except, in fact, it's a skill that comes into play in ordinary life.

Negotiating in Everyday Life: The Little Victories that Horseplay

Take a simple example: sharing a utility bill with a roommate.

Someone could insist that they split the costs evenly. Others, who travel frequently and use little electricity, might think that's unfair. Rather than allowing frustration to fester, they can also explain their rationale, propose alternatives such as paying for what they use, and negotiate a resolution that effectively shares the difference.

It's not "winning" the conversation — it's about making sure everything stays fair and avoiding needless conflict. The same applies to:

Relationships often involve budgets. One person likes to spend on experiences (travel, dining out) and the other is the saver. Finding a middle ground allows them to savor life's pleasures while also attaining financial stability.

Takes skill to negotiate with service providers. If you know what to ask for, you can sometimes negotiate cable bills, mobile plans, and even rent.

Negotiation is crucial when making significant purchases. Whether you're negotiating a price to buy the car or rent the apartment, learning how to negotiate can save you thousands in the long run.

A successful negotiation builds your confidence. And that confidence can apply to much larger financial decisions.

CAREER & FINANCIAL GROWTH: KNOW YOUR VALUE

Negotiation skills are crucial in the office environment.

Many accept the first salary offer they receive, thinking there's no room for pushbacks. But in most cases, there is. Negotiation is an expected part of the process for candidates.

Good salary negotiation, for instance, can result in better pay and benefits or more flexible work arrangements!

Negotiating rates for freelancing or side-hustle work provides protection against underpayment.

Even broaching the subject of promotion timelines with a boss can put you on a faster growth trajectory.

The key is knowing how to display your worth, supporting it with evidence, and standing strong without being aggressive.

Financial Planning: Making Yourself an Offer You Can't Refuse

Apart from dealing with others, negotiation is key in personal finance. The hardest person to negotiate with, sometimes, is yourself.

Think about it:

You want to save, but you also want to live. A strict budget can seem limiting, but it is also neither sustainable nor necessary to spend forever. Discovering common ground means spending on what is truly important.

Finding a way to pay off debt can be daunting. Many may not realize it, but loan terms, interest rates, and payment schedules can often be renegotiated — whether it's an education loan or a credit card balance.

Investing in the long term requires trade-offs. More risk usually delivers more reward, but how much uncertainty are you willing to tolerate?

The ability to negotiate between the instant gratification of short-term desires and the long-term goals people have been what differentiates those that are financially successful.

HOW TO IMPROVE AT NEGOTIATION: BUILDING THE RIGHT MINDSET

Not comfortable negotiating? Start small.

- Train in less stressed scenarios. Negotiate for a better rate on gym membership or ask for a minor discount at a local shop. The worst they can say is no.

- Learn to listen. Negotiation is not only about talking to others but also about understanding their needs.

- Do your research. Understanding the numbers, whether it's salary, rent, or interest rates, gives you an advantage.

- Be flexible but firm. Good negotiation means both sides should feel they've gotten something.

- Know when to walk away. You shouldn't pursue every deal. The best move in a negotiation is sometimes to simply say, "This isn't right for me."

Final thoughts — The Power of Negotiation for Your Financial Independence

At its heart, negotiation isn't about the best deal — it's about the right deal. The deal should be equitable, sustainable, and aligned with your financial goals.

The essential ability to negotiate well means:

- Less wasteful spending.

- More money and careers.

- Smarter financial choices.

- Fairer foundation for better relationships.

Negotiating is just as much a lesson for young adults entering financial independence as saving or investing. Ultimately, your approach to financial discussions can shape your entire future.

EXPRESSING ASSERTIVENESS AND EMPATHY

Discussing money can be complicated. From splitting a bill to negotiating a salary to setting boundaries with friends, financial conversations need both confidence and sensitivity. Too assertive? You risk sounding selfish. Too empathetic? You may become a target.

So how do you find the right balance?

Guilt-Free Speaking Up Assertiveness

Imagine you're out to dinner with some friends. The bill comes, and someone proposes splitting it evenly. But all you ordered was a salad and water — while everyone else had cocktails and appetizers. Do you keep quiet and pay more than your share? Or do you speak up?

Being assertive simply is saying how you feel about something in a straightforward, confident manner — without being a jerk about it. You might say:

"Oh, I just had a little snack. Would you mind if I did my part separately?"

No anger. No defensiveness. Just a simple, honest statement."

Why does this matter? Moreover, a lack of clarity in communication can lead to misunderstandings. If you never voice your discomfort, other people might assume you are fine with the arrangement. Over time that can wrought resentment or unneeded financial strain."

Set the Setting — Empathy: how to relate to others but not forget about You

Now, consider the alternative scenario. A friend cannot afford their rent. They don't mention it, but you notice that they've been ignoring group outings with increasing frequency and finding excuses not pitch in on shared expenses.

Rather than hastily concluding that they are neglecting their responsibilities, empathy enables you to comprehend the broader situation. Perhaps they have just lost a freelance job. Perhaps family expenses are increasing.

Sometimes a simple check-in makes all the difference:

"Hey, I've seen you've been a bit quiet about rent this month. Is everything okay?"

This is not about offering to pay for their half — it's about recognizing their circumstances and helping them to find a solution together.

It's easier to solve problems when financial conversations include empathy. Perhaps you agree to temporarily limit certain expenses or assist them in brainstorming ways to work within a budget. The key is to strike a balance without jeopardizing your own financial stability.

Everyday Scenarios Where Balance Matters

♦ Group Travel Planning: Some friends want luxury stays, some budget trip. Negotiate a plan that works for everyone instead of allowing anger to fester.

♦ Shared Living Costs: One roommate runs the AC constantly, while another rarely spends time at home. End resentment over utility bills with fairer conversations.

♦ Salary Negotiation: Few employees disclose their best number first. Being assertive is asking for better pay. Knowing the company's limitations and negotiating smart? That's empathy.

- Loan Repayments & Family Expectations: A lot of young adults feel the need to support family financially. It is important to balance helping family with helping yourself.

How to Get Better at This Balance

- Start with small Talks — Initiate casual conversation, for instance, by inquiring about a discount or dividing up some bill with your friends.

- Sometimes, it's important to pay attention to what someone is not saying, just as important as what they are saying.

- Be Direct, Not Hostile - Assertiveness doesn't mean being adversarial — you want to be understood, not to vanquish.

- Be Aware of Your Limits — Being nice doesn't mean jeopardizing your financial stability.

- Review Past Conversations — Were there any times you stayed silent when you should have spoken up? Did you overdo it in a conversation with someone? Learn from each experience.

A balance is where the strength lies

Assertiveness without consideration can be icy. And for the opposite reason, being empathetic without being assertive to the extreme will, in the end, make one feel robbed and exploited.

But together? They induce a mental state that will empower you to conduct financial discourse with confidence, fairness, and authority. And that's a skill that pays, both in money and in meaning, for life.

FINAL THOUGHTS

Integrating this discipline requires the ability to communicate effectively and engage with others. In this chapter, we've discussed how by practicing active listening, we lay the groundwork for mutual trust and understanding in financial conversations, paving the way for better choices. By listening carefully to others' points of view, recent graduates and young adults learn to make decisions around shared expenses or potential investments more clearly. This includes the ability to confidently communicate your needs and establish clear boundaries, preventing misguided or overextended decisions that could potentially lead to financial constraints.

Furthermore, the mix of being assertive with empathy makes one better suited to handling sensitive financial issues. Empathy can help to frame conversations about money in a compassionate way, realizing that each peer or family member has a different background and set of circumstances. Finding this balance builds relationships and encourages collaborative problem-solving, where everyone involved feels heard and valued. With practice, you will start to incorporate these skills into your day-to-day conversations, making more responsible decisions that are compatible with your values and goals, and as a result, being the architect of your long-term financial well-being and freedom.

Chapter 8

PSYCHOLOGICAL ASPECTS OF FINANCE

Psychological factors in finance uncover unknown forces that impact financial behavior and often shape decisions more than we would expect. These drivers change every part of how people handle money, from impromptu buys to long-term investments. Understanding the psychology behind these aspects gives us insight into why people may pull out their credit cards when the impulse strikes or derive satisfaction from watching their savings stack up. This chapter delves into the emotional pathways that influence financial behavior, offering fascinating insights into how the mind can navigate various complex pathways to shape our financial behavior.

This chapter takes a step away from the numbers and strategies of finance to explore the emotional and cognitive forces at play in these decisions. It deals with the influence of fear, comparison, and gratification delay on spending behavior, most especially with young adults and new graduates who are dealing with societal pressures and market complexities. Readers will be introduced to how social media instills anxieties like FOMO (Fear of Missing Out) and causes impulsive buying. It will also look at how mindfulness and conscious decision-making can serve as antidotes to these tendencies, cultivating financially healthy habits that support their values. The goal is to give readers awareness of the biases that drive their decisions and how their emotions affect money behaviors so that they can make choices more intentionally.

EFFECTS OF FOMO AND SOCIAL COMPARISON

Explain The FOMO Effect: How Social Media Shapes Spending Habits

Money decisions are never merely about numbers. They're emotional. Today's world, driven by Instagram, TikTok, and endless curated feeds, has influenced our financial emotions more than before.

For adolescents and recent grads alike, the pressure to "keep up" is tangible. The fear of missing out, or FOMO, and social comparison have become strong motivators for how people spend, whether it's on the newest phone, a luxury holiday, or a hot new restaurant.

But at what cost?

Fear of Missing Out (FOMO) Drives Us to Spend on a Whim

Ever seen a buddy post about an impromptu escape? Or a group shot from a concert you missed due to the ticket price? That gut-punched sensation — as though you've missed out on the highest quality moments of life — is FOMO in action.

Social media feeds curate everything and make it look exciting, seamless, effortless, and, above all, accessible. It's tempting to think, "Everyone else is doing it, so why shouldn't I?" And just like that, you've convinced yourself that charging that unplanned expense is completely justified.

The reality?

What you are seeing is, for the most part, meticulously curated. That "easy" vacation may land on someone's credit card for months.

Comparison isn't fair. You don't get the complete financial story, only the highlights.

The cycle never stops. There is always another trip, another gadget, and another trend. I mean, if you keep pursuing, it never stops.

Keeping Up vs. Keeping Sane: The Social Pressure to Spend

FOMO is only part of the story. The other is social comparison.

When scrolling through social media, humans inherently compare their lives to those of others. That's human nature. But with money, this habit can be perilous.

Your friend is getting a new iPhone? You have no idea whether they paid cash or availed themselves of an EMI for two years.

The pair is splurging on an expensive meal every weekend. Perhaps they are withholding rent and living in style.

The one in the designer outfit? Someone might sponsor it, borrow it, or simply live beyond their means.

The issue isn't that people want nice things. It's that we tend to pursue lifestyles without grasping the actual price.

Freedom From FOMO: How to Avoid Allowing Your Finances to Be Controlled By FOMO

The good news? You can take back control. Here's how:

Pause Before You Spend

The next time you want to buy something because of what you saw online, stop. Ask yourself:

Do I want this, or do I want it just because I saw somebody else had it?

Will this purchase make me happy a month from now?

Can I do this without feeling guilty or going into debt?

Reflection can distinguish between mindfulness and impulse spending.

Curate Your Social Media

Your mindset is influenced by your feeding. If you're constantly scrolling past luxury lifestyles and extravagant spending, it's only natural to feel inadequate.

Unfollow people who make you feel like you need to spend more than you have.

Budgeting and mindful spending pages.

When you feel financially stretched, limit your time on social media.

Even small adjustments in what you consume online can be a step toward a shift in your financial mindset.

Set Your Own Financial Goals

Forget what others are doing. What do YOU want?

Do you want to be debt-free?

Save for an exotic vacation, without stress?

Establish an emergency fund so you never have to fret about money?

By defining your own financial priorities, it will be easier to say no to needless spending. Because that fast rupee saved is a near miss to something potentially much bigger when your money has a cause.

Create a "FOMO Budget"

Let's be honest, you don't have to avoid everything.

Set aside a portion of your income for spontaneous activities such as attending a concert, taking a weekend trip, or occasionally treating yourself to a fancy dinner.

This will allow you to embrace life and not undermine your financial future.

Talk Openly About Money

Discuss financial issues with your friends. You'd be surprised — a lot of people feel the same pressure and don't discuss it.

When we destigmatize talking about money, budgeting and financial hardship, it becomes easier to press back against peer pressure.

The Bottom Line: Prioritize Financial Freedom Over Social Pressure

At the end of the day, true success isn't about how much you can spend, but rather about how much control you have over your money.

One moment of FOMO-fueled spending might provide a brief high. But long-term financial health? That's real peace of mind.

Spend wisely. Live intentionally. And remember — you aren't competing with anyone but yourself.

DELAYED GRATIFICATION

Delayed gratification is the bedrock of financial stability. This concept may be a little daunting yet very rewarding for a host of young adults in the country, especially for those who are just college students starting their financial journey or fresh graduates stepping into the industry. The economics of lifestyle choices, arguably the most fundamental skill in personal finance, revolves around the ability to postpone gratification to achieve better long-term results.

Not the same as saying "no" to an impulse buy, delayed gratification is an understanding of how those little choices compound over time. Imagine deciding whether to buy the latest technology in the form of a smartphone or to task your money into a savings option. Though the smartphone promises instant gratification, a few months of saving that money will eventually add up to a noble amount, which gives you some reassurance and freedom over time. Such a mindset is crucial to creating a rich life — it helps people to manage their finances effectively by staying away from the allure of instant gratification through expenditure while preparing for a brighter future.

Deferred gratification offers psychological benefits beyond mere financial gain. Those who practice delayed gratification develop emotional resilience by placing long-term goals ahead of instant gratification. Patience and Less Stress — People who develop kindness can stress out less about their financial situation. Financial anxiety is widespread among young adults these days, particularly when social norms dictate we can afford to maintain certain lifestyles. The second magical benefit of delayed gratification is that it restores a sense of control, makes stress less of a challenge, and increases financial security.

There are many tactics for building delayed gratification into your financial life. Determining specific financial goals is a priority. These can vary from shorter-term objectives, like saving up for a laptop, to bigger targets like home ownership or retirement. Having clearly defined goals gives us direction and motivates us to pursue them, which in turn makes it easier to avoid spontaneous spending.

Savings plans adapted to needs and capabilities form a different pillar for cultivating delayed gratification. These can include automatic transfers to a savings account, regularly allocating a percentage of one's salary every month, or using budgeting tools to ensure meticulous record-keeping of expenditure. A structured savings method, such as investing in a Treasury bond or short-term bond ETF, enables individuals to gradually build their reserves, which can be monitored through statements and fosters the patience necessary to achieve significant financial objectives.

A good strategy that many people say works well for them is to add 'waiting period' before making purchases. If the impulse to buy something unnecessary strikes, leaving time to pass from the moment of desire—be it one day, one week, or one month—can serve to see if that desire remains. It's common that needs that felt urgent don't hold over time, and people make better financial choices that fit their goals.

Apart from individual habits, larger cultural messages about instant gratification also play a major role in financial decisions. In our competitive and fast-paced world, where social media praises instant results and consumption, there is some underlying pressure to live up to these ideals. But reframing success from immediate to sustained can shift your narrative of winning. This shows that patience not only leads to wealth accumulation but also makes the culture more impatient, greedy, desperate for wealth, etc.

Encouraging delayed gratification can also change the way that success is defined and achieved. Long-term impact and personal achievement measure success, not material possessions or glamorized lifestyles. It helps people who want to achieve their goals appreciate the process instead of being focused on the outcomes, so they can lead to more sustainable success instead of just moments.

Youth, new professionals, and scholars acknowledge and use delayed gratification to understand its implications on fashion, lifestyle, and mental health. If they shifted their focus to financial education that promotes delayed gratification, it could change how the younger generations manage their money

Vignettes of successful people with a practice of delayed gratification would be highly motivating. Real-world examples and results, where entrepreneurs, investors, or everyday people prioritize long-term gains and success over immediate gratification, serve as compelling narratives of true patience in action. These stories can encourage others to develop the same habits, thus acting as a powerful reminder of the physical rewards of delaying gratification.

UNDERSTANDING FINANCIAL STRESS

Life in our 20s can be tough and financially challenging. A common mismatch between income and expenditures among young adults can significantly impact their mental health. In fact, someone recently graduating and beginning their first job may experience that their pay cannot satisfy all of their needs, like rent, food, and transportation. This discrepancy results in a persistent sense of anxiety as they strive to meet their financial obligations, settle their student loans, and reduce their credit card debt.

Financial-related stress has deep psychological effects. Chronic exposure to stress can cause anxiety, depression, and even physical health issues. Stress reduces a person's enjoyment of leisure due to financial difficulties, which can negatively impact social relationships and overall life satisfaction. As individuals grapple with $95,000 debt on average and must work two or three jobs just to pay these debts, their self-worth—too often tied to their bank account balance—can suffer and lead to feelings of powerlessness or failure. Much of the time, people end up stuck in a situation where there seems to be no way out, where they can't escape being stressed, because their financial condition is not shifting.

Societal pressure compounds financial stress by setting unrealistic standards of lifestyles. In a time where our lives are so heavily molded by what we put out on social media, it can feel like we owe it to ourselves to uphold a certain quality of life. Young adults might feel it is a pressure to buy what they show on vacation, luxury things, or eat at expensive restaurants. Risky financial behaviors, such as overspending or incurring debt to maintain an unaffordable lifestyle, commonly accompany this compulsion. Instead of following basic needs, people start spending more on nonessential things or on affordability, leading to increased financial instability.

Chronic financial stress can limit decision-making capacity — trapping people in a spiral. This chronic stress disrupts cognitive function, resulting in incorrect decisions such as not paying the bills or forgetting to set aside money for emergencies. Stress clouds the mind, making it difficult to evaluate financial options critically, which can result in costly loans or unfavorable investments. Impaired decision-making can result in a vicious cycle, as stress can cause poor financial decisions and increase anxiety. This phenomenon can then become a long-term cycle of debts and insecurity, with all that entails in terms of personal feeling and loss of control, eventually becoming overwhelming and distressing.

Building financial literacy and developing a supportive network can be proactive steps in managing financial stress. Being financially literate means that one has knowledge about budgeting, saving, and investing, which allows individuals to make informed choices that mesh well with their economic goals. Having some knowledge about financial principles creates a better work-life balance for young adults to create realistic budgets and stay in their own lanes instead of borrowing debt. Many employers, schools, and community organizations offer financial education programs that can help provide useful advice on how to be smart with money.

In addition, support networks help in reducing financial pressures. Spending time with peer groups, advisers, or groups in the community who know there is often a heavy mental component to financial management is also very helpful, both emotionally and with practical advice. By sharing experiences and strategies with others, it helps people understand that they are not alone in their struggles, decreasing the sense of isolation. Help networks can also link people to more asset help, be they educational facilities or loan program providers, providing some other sources of assistance

Guidelines run deep in helping prevent the backsliding of long-term discipline to short-term ease. Another helpful component is encouragement for young adults to create realistic financial goals as per their specific situations. It means determining what's possible financially instead of responding to outside forces pushing us to spend. This encourages more sustainable spending patterns because it focuses on what truly matters instead of what people tell you you should be doing with your money. If a few trips or a few more days of seeing family simply bring joy and fulfill that personal narrative, then budgeting for those periods and cutting back further on less important things can preserve financial security without needing to feel like they're making any sort of sacrifice.

INFLUENCE OF COGNITIVE BIASES

Understanding How Cognitive Biases Affect Financial Decision-Making — How to Beat Them

Money is rare, if ever; it's just a question of numbers. It's emotional. and often, the financial decisions we make around spending, saving, or investing are influenced by subconscious biases and not by

Understanding these biases can make a significant difference for young adults, including recent graduates and those entering financial independence, as it can determine whether they accumulate wealth or make regrettable mistakes. Here's a look at some of the most common cognitive biases involved in our financial choices — and how to avoid them.

1. **Confirmation Bias: Hearing Only What You Want to Hear**

   Did you ever feel strong about stocks, a cryptocurrency, or a business idea, and then seek out information that confirms you were right? This is an example of confirmation bias in action.

   Imagine that you were confident that one of the stocks would collapse, as it had in the past. You search for good news, dismiss red flags and ignore any advice from experts that contradicts your own hunches."

   The result? Concerned, will you overlook the key risks that cause poor investment decisions? Quiz yourself about which risks matter.

   How to Beat It:

   Challenge your assumptions. Before finalizing a decision, actively look for competing perspectives.

   Consider the opposing viewpoint. The question: "What will I pay if I'm wrong?"

   Diversify sources. Find multiple and trusted sources — don't believe social media or a single investment blog.

2. **Overconfidence Bias: Thinking You're Smarter Than the Market**

   Confidence is great. Overconfidence? Not so much.

   Many young investors are convinced they know better than their elders — whether that's timing the stock market, the crypto market or some combination of the two by thinking they understand complex financial products when they don't.

A recent graduate might put a significant part of her savings into high-risk stocks because she is convinced she has found the next Tesla or Bitcoin.

A first-time entrepreneur has no idea how much capital they will need to survive year one.

The problem? The financial chores can be brutal when reality falls short of expectations.

How to Beat It:

Know what you don't know. Not even experienced investors always forecast transitions correctly.

Test your knowledge. Try small ways to see what is working before you make any big moves

Listen to experts. They may not always be correct, but they are based on experience and can guide you.

3. **Loss Aversion: Fear of Letting Go**

Has everyone ever held onto a loser because you knew it had to come back? Or sold a stock too soon just to "lock in" a small gain?

That's loss aversion — that we feel worse about losing money than we feel positive about gaining it.

One reason is that investors cling to failing assets too long because selling them is a sign

One reason is that investors tend to hold onto failing assets for an extended period, as they perceive selling them as a sign of failure.

TRUE: People sell their winning stocks too early because they fear losing profits.

How to Beat It:

Set clear rules. Plan when you sell an investment (for gains or losses).

Think long-term. Do not make emotional decisions based on volatility in the short term.

Detach from past decisions. Buying something doesn't mean you have to keep it — if it is a mistake, take your loss and move on.

FEAR OF MISSING OUT & SOCIAL COMPARISON: SHOPPING TO "KEEP UP"

Social media compounds financial stress in ways earlier generations did not experience.

A buddy posts photos of a lavish vacation.

An influencer is flaunting their newest premium hardware.

Friends gloat over new cars, designer clothes or pricier food.

Feeling like you're losing ground can happen all too easily. And before you know it, you're spending money you don't have — simply to keep up.

How to Beat It:

Unfollow or mute triggers. If certain accounts leave you not good enough, curate your feeding.

Pause before purchases. Ask: Do I really want this? Or do I just want to look successful?

Just keep in mind, social media is not real life. As the saying goes, people don't share photos of their debt statements.

Anchoring Bias: Letting The First Number Define Your Thought Process

Ever seen a price of ₹10,000 on a product and then found out, wait, it's ₹5,000— and paying that feels like a steal?

That's anchoring bias. If the original price was ₹12,000, anything would seem like a massive discount even as the fair price might have always been ₹5,000.

This bias affects:

Retail shopping: "Was ₹2,000, now only ₹999!"

How salary negotiations go: The first number an employer puts on the table is what sets the number that comes next.

Real estate: A high listing price makes a small discount look bigger.

How to Beat It:

Ignore the first number. Consider: I am now prepared to pay how much for this?

Do your research. For instance, price, salaries, or market value drive decisions.

How to Improve Your Financial Decision-Making

Just because you know about these biases doesn't mean you won't ever succumb to them. However, it does empower you to scrutinize your financial choices before making hasty decisions.

Here's how to perfect your proficiency:

♦ Pause before big decisions.

   Before you invest, spend a single dollar, or incur a debt, ask yourself: Are there any biases at play?

♦ Be willing to collaborate with individuals from different perspectives.

   Talk to people whose thinking differs from yours as much as you do to people who agree with you.

♦ Set financial goals.

   Knowing your priorities (saving a house, building up an emergency fund, etc.) helps you resist emotional spending that much easier.

♦ Learn continuously.

The better informed you are financially, the less prone you are to the cognitive traps.

Closing Thought: Master Your Mind, Master Your Money

It all boils down to you" you want to earn, spend, invest; we know by now that the finances are no longer about 'the more the better', but "the smarter; and all of this is in the hand of you.

Your mind will always find ways to process your emotional, irrational decisions. The key is recognizing when that's happening — and removing yourself before you act.

When you own your money rather than having it own you, you can achieve true financial freedom.

Role of Emotional Intelligence in Finance

In fact, mood and stress management were a critical component to maintaining financial control, especially for young adults and new grads experiencing the trials of financial independence. Simply put, emotional intelligence is the ability to recognize and regulate your feelings and to understand other people's emotions. Applied to finance, this becomes a superpower, allowing us to manage financial worries better and make decisions that match our bigger picture.

The main advantage of high emotional intelligence is that it helps manage financial stress. Financial stress can stem from numerous sources, ranging from unexpected expenses, debt, or job insecurity. In India, young adults face a lot of societal pressure, and emotional intelligence is helpful for them to navigate through all the challenges they encounter. "Being able to identify that you're feeling stressed or anxious about money helps you take the step of addressing those feelings before you make poor decisions," she says. Recognizing and processing these emotions allows you to step back, contemplate the situation with logic, and determine the best route forward without stress dictating your moves.

Emotional intelligence enhances decision-making processes because it cultivates a deeper awareness of emotions. We're emotional, but we rarely factor it into our spending habits, which explains those impulse burdens we later regret. A major part of EI is recognizing your emotional triggers — stress, boredom, or social pressure — that can lead to such decisions. For example, people are likely to spend money on things they do not need when under pressure or purchase the latest electronic gadgets for social acceptance. Fortunately, high emotional intelligence enables individuals to recognize these triggers and, as a result, take a moment to reflect on whether they need the purchase. This intentional method helps you spend in a much more mindful way that makes sure you're making financial decisions out of logic, not emotion.

In addition, high emotional intelligence can help people resist both internal and external temptations, leading to greater control over personal finance. When recent graduates enter the workforce, they often face peer pressure to maintain a certain lifestyle due to social media depictions and cultural expectations around self-fulfillment. This is where emotional intelligence becomes crucial. It provides them with the tools that they need to resist these pressures and focus on their own financial priorities instead. As one develops the ability to have empathy and be self-aware, one finds ways to reinforce the idea to oneself and others that the idea of matching up spending with one's values is more gratifying than keeping up with outside expectations. Not only does this way of thinking create economic relevance, but it also reinforces your faith in your financial actions.

Building emotional intelligence is an ongoing process that consists mainly of three key components: self-awareness, empathy, and self-regulation. These all contribute in different ways to better financial decisions. Self-awareness is about exercising awareness of one's emotional state and how that translates into financial behavior. It inspires consideration of previous financial choices, recognizing trends or errors stemming from emotional response. Over time, as one develops increased self-awareness, they become better positioned to predict their emotional responses to future financial decisions to make more calculated, mindful decisions.

Another key ingredient of EI is empathy, and this deepens financial management through self and other emphasis. Empathy allows for consideration of the expected emotional response to financial decisions within the self as well as with other stakeholders. Considering money from this perspective encourages individuals to adopt responsible and ethical spending habits, prompting them to reconsider the distinction between wants and needs, as well as the implications of their financial choices.

The concept of self-regulation, which refers to the ability to manage and control one's emotions, is an essential building block needed to develop financial discipline. Self-regulation teaches people not to act on the immediate impulse to make a snap financial decision based on temporary emotions, such as excitement during a sale or panic when facing unexpected expenses. Instead, they develop patience and foresight and pursue long-term financial goals rather than seeking instant gratification. It is this discipline that enhances financial wellness and helps one cope with difficult financial times with poise, confidence, and aplomb.

SUMMARY AND REFLECTIONS

Young adults and new graduates are struggling with mental strain on their finances in today's reality. This chapter looks at the emotional determinants of finance habits — FOMO, social comparison, and the short-term emotional reward that triggers impulsiveness in spending. Understanding these influences allows individuals to better appreciate how these pressures society puts upon them or how they feel they have an impact on their financial decisions.

Understanding these mental factors is key in creating conscious spending patterns that are based on your priorities, not the latest crazes. By implementing concrete strategies, such as mindfulness practices and creating defined financial goals, young individuals can reduce the temptation to consume in the moment, promoting a lifetime of prudent financial decisions.

In addition, recognizing cognitive biases and improving emotional intelligence are important tools to deal with finances properly. Cognitive biases—such as confirmation bias or overconfidence—regularly disrupt rational decision-making, leading to incorrect financial decisions. Likewise, this emotional intelligence enables individuals to respond differently to their financial needs and avoid making financial decisions that stem from emotional stimuli, equipping them to handle financial stress. These skills give them the ability to resist the pressures of media and society and develop resilience in their financial lives. By prioritizing authentic accomplishments over instant gratification, the practice of delayed retirement aligns values with a long-term financial strategy, nurturing a paradigm of barriers being smashed over blind success. This helps prepare youth to engage in and manage the changing realities of a financially complex world and creates a new understanding of creditworthiness in its myriad forms.

Chapter 9

RESOURCES FOR FINANCIAL LITERACY

Financial literacy is the cornerstone of sound financial decision-making throughout a lifetime. For young adults in India, financial education is not a skill but a tool for navigating adulthood with confidence. The leap from the haven of academia to the outside world brings about stark financial realities. Many college students find themselves caught between spending money and limited income, while recent graduates are grappling with the weight of debt. During such times, a proficient grasp of personal finance is imperative. The goal of this chapter is to showcase tools that make these people more aware and informed about their financial situation and to give them the power to implement their knowledge.

This chapter will introduce readers to various tools that can improve their financial literacy. We shall discover how lists and podcasts are ongoing learning tools that offer relatable stories and expert advice to lean into. Books can provide in-depth explorations of financial principles, encouraging young people to reassess how they approach managing money. Podcasts, meanwhile, provide continual education in an easy-to-consume format. Exploration: We will also explore digital platforms such as blogs and online articles, providing current and various viewpoints on financial issues. Audiobooks and TED Talks act as levers for engagement that bring these abstract concepts to life as much through auditory and visual learning as through text. In doing so, these resources provide readers with knowledge and insights critical to succeeding on the pathway to financial independence and stability in an increasingly fast-moving world.

READING LISTS AND PODCASTS FOR DEEPER LEARNING

As financial decisions spill into every part of life today, it is a must for young people to construct a strong base of financial literacy. The young adults in India who are either in college or have recently graduated find themselves in the complex situation of juggling their expenditure and debts while interests push them to spend money that they do not have. A library of credible resources that provide help and explanation is essential for starting the mission. In this list of resources, I would wager that books and podcasts are among the most vital tools that can help people learn about personal finance well into the future.

Books, as timeless repositories of wisdom, offer the fundamental knowledge necessary for prudent financial management. Consider classics like "Rich Dad Poor Dad," by Robert Kiyosaki, or "The Total Money Makeover," by Dave Ramsey. These texts have served as guides for the eager for decades, offering strategies for budgeting, debt repayment, and wealth building. Not only do they teach, but they motivate people to reevaluate how they view money while providing detailed explanations of intricate concepts in digestible advice. Books provide the unique gift of exploration. A single volume can delve into intricate details, revealing layer after layer of information that prompts us to consider the merits of acting.

In the Indian economy, with its myriad contexts, attention to literature that accommodates a variety of voices and perspectives in this space is important. Financial stories from a variety of backgrounds provide a wider perspective for readers, representing different cultures and economic systems. This literature prepares you for financial and global challenges. All perspectives are helpful to a certain extent; having different viewpoints can help people understand more and combine information in a way that works best for them. It improves one's comprehension of financial terms, turning what once seemed like jargon into a natural understanding.

Injecting oneself with streams of financial literature and not just passive text puts people on a proactive spiral. Consuming financial content on a regular basis strengthens the mind, like how working a muscle strengthens it. Readers become instinctive-oriented and develop foresight for the financial implications of trends. This isn't simply a matter of information consumption but rather of information interaction which will use questioning of ideas and make them part of our life strategy. It is the habit of never-ending learning that makes sure that one keeps up with the fast-paced changes of the economic world.

Apps and websites, similarly, have boomed alongside popular finance podcasts, which have spiked in popularity by providing ongoing education courtesy of relatable experiences and interviews with experts. Shows like "The Dave Ramsey Show" or "Freakonomics Radio" add life to financial concepts, making them easily digestible for even the busiest of individuals. When listened to on the go or in spare time, these conversations turn wasted moments into growth moments. Podcasts utilize an element of storytelling, showcasing real-world scenarios that potential listeners may one day find themselves in. This format helps even difficult subjects feel relevant and encourages listeners to practice the lessons they hear.

Podcasts even bring in the voices of finance experts and influence the areas. A wealth of knowledge built from experience and years in practice through interviews with financial advisors, economists, and entrepreneurs. Having direct access to industry expertise is crucial for young adults or fresh graduates looking for guidance. Learning about successes and failures firsthand gives a personal touch to the learning experience, demonstrating that the road to financial sustainability is not easy but can be charted.

Additionally, the episodic format of podcasts means that listeners are treated to a continuous stream of information; it helps them stay up to date on all the emerging trends and strategies. This can be especially useful in the fast-moving world of finance, where new developments can change the landscape overnight. A better understanding makes it easier to manage personal wealth and to be ready to capitalize on the latest developments.

Highlighting the significance of these resources is their capacity to reroute the young adults' and pupils' mindset about money. It involves confidence and a sense of empowerment and includes the lesson that financial independence is an achievable goal. Whether you click through a book on a lazy afternoon or listen to a podcast on an early morning jog, each engagement adds to a corpus of knowledge.

Engaging with books and podcasts can make the difference between financial adolescence and adulthood. By studying the various trajectories of policies such as taxation, they also prepare one to not only confront challenges squarely but also to be able to anticipate and avoid potential pitfalls before they materialize.

BLOGS, ONLINE ARTICLES, AUDIOBOOKS, AND TED TALKS

In a world where most facets of life have gone digital, the internet has emerged as a powerful tool for young adults working toward becoming financially literate. There are so many online tools that it's easy to find lifestyle-related content. A major category of these resources is blogs. These platforms serve as a goldmine of trends and relatable content in the present as well as stories that are very similar to those of young adults figuring out their finances.

Blogs serve not only as resources but also as an encouraging platform enabling people to learn about money management. They instead provide unique insights into real-life problems and eventual successes, which avoids the typical pitfalls or even inspires them to try them before embarking on their own strategy, which was previously inspired. A young professional, for example, may stumble onto the blog detailing one person's escape from student debt — not just practical advice, but an ally in the struggle through relatability. In short, blogs are a mirror of the changing financial world and a way for readers to feel connected.

Blogs are great, but online articles provide another engaging option to keep you up to date on new financial strategies. These expert-written (or well-researched journalist-written) articles give you current insight into economic trends, investment opportunities, budgeting techniques, and more. Access to reliable data is essential to making informed decisions that can impact your long-term goals, not just for college students starting on their financial journeys, but for everyone. Informative articles on subjects like how interest rates work or how to select various types of savings accounts give young adults the basic knowledge they need to empower themselves to tackle money obstacles with confidence.

Additionally, the conciseness of many online articles makes them easy to digest and perfect for recent graduates who are often balancing work and other responsibilities. This accessibility not only keeps young adults up to date with crucial financial news but also minimizes the time investment required. Instead of consuming it all at once, they can repeatedly expose themselves to this kind of content and gradually develop a strong knowledge base related to finance over time.

Audiobooks, which fit so well with a modern lifestyle, are also accessible. These enable personnel to learn important concepts on the flight. When commuting, exercising, or doing chores becomes so common, audiobooks enable flexibility and comfort by incorporating these moments into lessons.

When commuting, exercising, or doing chores becomes so common, audiobooks enable flexibility and comfort by incorporating these moments into lessons. Whether it's learning how to budget effectively or understanding the intricacies of the stock market, audiobooks are comprehensive and don't demand your full focus on a screen. If you struggle to maintain focus while reading, listening can help you retain information better.

Audiobooks allow you to turn the otherwise idle time that makes up much of your life into opportunities for learning. For example, a young adult can spend his/her morning commute learning about basic investments, thus maximizing his/her time while naturally embedding financial education in their life.

Learning becomes the consumption of information in virtually real time, followed by reinforcing beneficial behaviors toward independence through financial literacy. When it comes to money and personal development, TED Talks are a fantastic option in addition to written (blog posts and eBooks) and audio (podcasts) formats.

These TED Talks feature networked speakers and shooting format, resulting in motivational speeches that will make you reconsider how to plan your finances. They occasionally include experts who discuss groundbreaking and transformative approaches to finance, investing, and achieving a lower degree of freedom.

A TED Talk on behavioral economics, for instance, might discuss how psychological triggers affect the way we spend and save. These kinds of discussions can be some of the most intricate concepts in a simple and fair manner, inspiring curiosity and a call to action. Incorporating personal tales and professional observations, TED Talks present storytelling and expert commentary in a cohesive form — one that serves simultaneously as entertainment and education to inspire viewers to rethink their own circumstances and put their newfound knowledge to use.

With young adults being subject to society's pull towards spending and the complexities of debt after graduating, utilizing an array of online resources is key to building financial literacy. Overall, these tools offer a comprehensive approach to personal finance education, addressing various learning styles and preferences. Websites, online books, audio books, and TED Talks can all be used as invaluable tools in an individual's quest to become financially literate.

FREE AND PAID ONLINE COURSES

How: Golf: In fact, faster — digital, personal, and finance: It became something to learn. Financial independence and stability are the first steps for every young adult leaving college and entering a competitive job market in India with monthly salaries. You have the option to self-study these topics, but it's always beneficial to have a structured approach, as demonstrated in online courses. These courses cover a wide range of financial management topics, as most individuals can afford them. Financial literacy online courses have plenty of advantages, with availability being the most evident. With so many options for every budget, students of all types can find something.

However, there are several existing platforms that offer free courses for students and children to learn at no extra charge. Free options do cover fundamental concepts — budgeting, credit, for example — that give people a solid place to start learning about personal finance.

For more depth, more expertise, and more time paid-for courses are available. These, again, can be full-fledged guides to complex subjects or niche ones, like investment strategies or tax strategies. With both free and paid courses available, students can determine what level of time and money they can, and want, to spend and, therefore, create a pathway that is most valuable to them in the end." This flexibility also guarantees that financial literacy reaches everyone, regardless of cost barriers.

While a course aids in diversifying a credible knowledge system, the best course platform is also an instrumental factor to consider. Generally, reputable institutions and credentialed professionals conduct these courses, enhancing their credibility and ensuring students receive accurate and up-to-date information. Confidence through Familiarity — When learners understand that they are studying from materials created by reputable resources, it instills an assurance in their education. And trust is key to that relationship in order to be able to put those financial principles into action in one's daily life — and let it also guide one's own life. such as retirement savings, for instance."

Many of these courses also offer completion certificates. These are credentials that start with the learner and show that they have specific knowledge and would therefore be beneficial to their résumé and knowledge. That means having the knowledge of financial literacy can put you in the lead. And, can you even imagine from the very moment that someone will be entering into the corporate job (or even hourly) and then only the HR would say, "You did so great in your Practical Finance!" And you are going to be blessed with a 10%, even a 20% salary bonus? So, a favorable course certification from a known person may help a job seeker as well as a person working today.

Students can explore a wide range of topics in the online classes, ranging from basic topics such as saving and investing to more complex topics such as cryptocurrency and behavioral finance. The content is so diverse, learners can chart their own path based on their interests and objectives. "You're putting your learning into some kind of human context, to other people that actually are doing what you do, and it's much more interactional, and it allows people to tailor it around the things that are important for their life and for their job."

Additionally, application in MOOCs is not only theory-focused but also practice-oriented with quizzes and case studies. These elements allow students to stay mindful of the theory and apply it in real-time situations. Whether they're simulating investments in the stock market or budgeting their own plans, these interactive aspects allow for much more responsive and resonant perspectives on finances.

By taking these courses, students not only learn to think critically about the various financial systems tied to a country but also how to navigate those systems competently. Budgeting, saving, investing, and debt management come naturally over time, instilling financial literacy in people and ultimately ensuring that individuals make prudent choices regarding their finances. That is liberating, especially for young adults who believe they have to spend and new graduates who brave the world facing student debt and other liabilities.

These are four-week programs, also ethereal, providing unparalleled multiplicity. Students learn at their own pace, repeating concepts they find difficult and accelerating through material they already understand. This is especially useful for busy college students or employees who want to develop a way of learning that works for them and their timetable. After preparing, these endeavors have manifested in various forms, some of which are related to their responsibilities.

COURSE TOPICS AND SPECIALIZATIONS

How Online Courses Teach Young Adults to Take Control of Their Finances

Most people do not learn money management in school. However, upon entering the real world, young adults face the challenge of managing rent, bills, savings, investments, and debt without a clear plan. This is where online financial courses can be useful.

These classes are not simply about dry textbook theories. They provide actionable strategies that can be applied in real life. Whether you're seeking to control your spending, begin investing, or strategizing for retirement, a course is available to assist you.

Step One: Learning the Basics

For beginners, search for courses that will offer you small, actionable steps for budgeting, saving, and debt management.

- ◆ Track Income & Expenses – Where is your money really going?
- ◆ Financial Goals — Saving for a laptop, a holiday, or an emergency fund.
- ◆ Smart Saving Habits – Set up automatic savings and eliminate wasteful spending.

Knowing how to rein in expenditure and establish savings is the basis of financial independence. A robust budget plan prevents financial regret in the future.

Beyond the Basics: Learning To Build Wealth

Once you've mastered the day-to-day, the next step is making your money work for you.

- Investment Courses: Commercial stocks, bonds, mutual funds, and real estate What's smart? What's risky? What's the way you evaluate an investment?

- Passive Income & Side Hustles – Many courses look at additional income streams, from freelancing to dividend investing.

- Market Fundamentals – Learning to read financial trends is key for long-term wealth building.

Investing might feel a bit scary when you first hear about it, but good courses break it down, showing you step-by-step how to get started on a small scale and scale up prudently.

Specialized Learning: Finance for Every Goal

Not every person needs the same financial literacy. That's part of the reason some online courses target financial goals:

- Salary Negotiation & Career Finance — Master higher pay, taxes, and earnings.

- Cryptocurrency & Emerging Markets – Interested in Bitcoin, NFTs, and decentralized finance? Some offerings explore the risks and opportunities in-depth.

- Home Ownership & Real Estate – Are you looking to buy a home? Understand mortgages, property valuation, and financing.

These more focused courses allow young adults to further specialize their financial education to meet their individual and career goals.

Why Online Learning Is So Effective

Online courses are more interactive than generic finance books. Many include:

- Quizzes & Exercises — To assess knowledge and reinforce important lessons.

- Real-Life Case Studies — Follow actual financial triumphs (and blunders).

- Simulated Budgets & Investments – Play in a safe environment.

Some platforms even provide discussion forums for students to network, ask questions, and share insights with one another. Having this community helps engage learners and holds them accountable.

Flexibility & Accessibility

The biggest advantage of online courses? You learn at your own pace.

- Busy with work or college? Prepare for an hour each day.

- Location doesn't matter. Study anywhere—from your house to a café, even your phone.

- Budget-friendly options. Most courses are free or serve as low-cost alternatives to pricey university classes.

This flexibility also makes financial education more easily accessible than ever, empowering anyone, regardless of income or background, to build the skills necessary for financial success.

Final Thoughts: Why Financial Education Matters

For young adults, and even recent graduates, learning money is no longer optional.

The cost of living is rising.

Loans and debts are common.

Investing at a young age will set you up for life.

Online courses provide an affordable, accessible way to learn these skills on your schedule. Whether you're looking to pay down debt, build wealth, or prepare for the future, time spent on financial literacy is one of the best investments you can make.

INTERACTIVE COMPONENTS AND COMMUNITY

The notion that financial knowledge gained through interactive means is much better resonates, especially in a world where online financial education is prevalent with so much information at their fingertips (young adults and recent graduates are just starting their financial journeys).

Quizzes and projects serve as a bridge between theory and practice. They provide an interactive means of reinforcing material covered, enabling users to challenge their grasp of financial principles, concepts, and procedures without any penalty for incorrect answers. For example, a quiz on budgeting methods asks learners to utilize what they have learned; the knowledge will become more concrete as well as memorable. Projects, by contrast, require participants to go beyond mere discussion and undertake richer investigative work, like when students build a pretend investment portfolio, a kind of case study in personal finance.

Another beneficial aspect of interactive financial education would be discussion boards. Such platforms function as discussion boards for collective learning, where users can post their insights, raise queries, and receive feedback from their peers as well as specialists. By getting input from others and sharing thoughts and perspectives, a community-learning ecosystem is created, which improves the effectiveness of learning. By talking about things like how to handle debt or how to save money, students can benefit from the collective knowledge of their peers, which leads to a deeper and more nuanced understanding of complicated financial issues.

Whether people are studying personal finance or are entirely focused on it, real-life case studies are effective ways to prepare students for real-life challenges in handling personal finances. Real-world cases help learners learn about the nuances and complexity involved in making financial decisions.

Real-world cases help learners learn about the nuances and complexity involved in making financial decisions. For instance, learning strategies that worked to successfully manage student loan repayment will bring recent graduates lessons that are relevant to their lives.

Communities provide the benefits of knowledge sharing, encouragement, and support throughout the entire learning process. When learners connect with other learners—by working on group projects, being part of a feedback session, or simply chit-chatting, they create a shared reservoir of knowledge that enriches the learning experience for all involved parties as far as financial concepts are concerned. For those experiencing societal pressures around topics like fitness, this space can be especially comforting to discuss challenges in an open manner and discover like-minded individuals with shared goals. From innovative saving techniques to investment opportunities, community-backed learning emboldens individuals to take control of their financial futures.

Interactive content is key to keeping participants engaged and maximizing the effectiveness of global financial education programs. Gamification and personalization features such as leaderboards and tailored feedback make the learning experience more relevant and rewarding to the user. Leaderboards can provide a competitive element to learning — helping keep users more engaged and invested. Gamification does the same to boring tasks where you must do a lot of things to work towards success; gamification will make that task exciting and enjoyable to do, encouraging a positive environment for learning. Generating practical feedback, an incorporated course to investigate the individuals who performed previously, can guarantee that they give constructive feedback, highlighting areas for improvement while also allowing them to build on their strengths.

These interactive components are guided by best practices for further enriching the learning experience. Educators and designers should strive to develop activities that are more straightforward and in line with the intended goals. Educators should design quizzes that assess learners' comprehension of essential concepts without overburdening them and develop projects that are both challenging enough to stimulate critical thinking and feasible enough to foster creativity. Discussion boards should be moderated to promote respectful, productive exchange, and real-life case studies need to feel relevant and up-to-date so as not to lose their audience.

Before adding this element, make sure your technology and resources can handle it. Making sure the online platforms are user-friendly and available over multiple devices is critical to ensure that learners from all walks of life can fully participate. Offering tutorials or introductory sessions on the proper use of these tools can prevent potential bottlenecks and enhance user confidence. This factor would boost accessibility among the young adults and college students who might be juggling many responsibilities and need their learning environment to be flexible.

In the end, interactive components of online financial education provide a lively method that educates and encourages action. Educators can create a rich tapestry of learning experiences that meet a variety of preferences by integrating quizzes, discussion boards, case studies, and community interactions. This makes financial concepts concrete, turning abstract theories into skills that can be applied in practice and enabling users to make informed decisions about their financial health.

FINAL THOUGHTS

In this chapter, we considered various resources for young adults and recent graduates in India to develop their financial literacy. Books offer timeless wisdom, while podcasts present real-life experiences and expert advice. Readers can adopt an active role in money management through reading different genres of books and listening to various money-related podcasts. Having this knowledge helps in making sound decisions when it comes to money; it will also serve as a sort of confidence builder, as an understanding of personal finance will make what can be a very complicated topic easier to manage with ease.

The chapter also emphasized the wealth of online resources available to anyone who wants guidance on their finances. Such resources include blogs, articles, audiobooks, and TED Talks, which aim to supplement conventional ways of learning by offering bite-sized, easy-to-use content that caters to contemporary daily lives. With free and paid online courses available, financial education is accessible to everyone, no matter their economic background. In summary, by combining various resources, young adults can learn with confidence as they transition into a world filled with the financial independence and capability needed to navigate an ever-changing financial system.

Chapter 10

TOOLS FOR ACHIEVING FINANCIAL FREEDOM

We would do it with a high-level understanding and tools, and external tools will ensure personal finance management in the end. Young Indian adults' journey to financial independence is filled with excitement and pressure from loved ones and the economic realities to which they were born. Therefore, armed with this information, you can develop disciplined monetary behaviors. This chapter surveys the types of interactive tools available that present the opportunity to provide a more automated approach to personal finance. The concept behind it is more of a paradigm shift, of approaches, systemic changes, and solutions that lead to ongoing and sustainable financial wellness.

This chapter talks about paradigms and tools that help to keep one's finances in check, such as the quizzes to know how financially fit one is, how to look for cost per feature and cost per functionality analysis, and how to set personal financial goals and achieve them. As a result, through breaking down these elements, the chapter seeks to provide college students and graduates with tangible ways to be fiscally responsible. We tailor the included material to not only cater to this unique audience but also to their specific needs, including debt management and employment transition. Interacting with the chapter will also teach you an impactful way to assess where someone is financially, which then gives insight on how to tailor financial actions according to where you want to go. The intent of this exploration is to inspire a move from reactive to proactive money management, establishing the groundwork for long-term financial prosperity and autonomy.

TOOLS FOR BUDGETING & EXPENSE TRACKING

Tracking income or expenses is one of the most important parts of maintaining cash flow management and wealth building.

1. **Budgeting Apps & Software**

   ◈ Walnut – Tracks expenses and categorizes spending.

   ◈ Money View – Helps manage finances and track transactions.

   ◈ ET Money – A comprehensive financial planning app.

   ◈ Google Pay & PhonePe – Monitor UPI transactions and set spending limits.

   ◈ YNAB (You Need a Budget) – Helps with proactive budgeting.

   ◈ Mint – Monitors spending and provides saving insights

   ◈ Excel/Google Sheets – To create your own budget templates.

   Budgeting Methods

   ◈ 50/30/20 Rule – 50% needs, 30% wants, 20% savings.

   ◈ Zero-Based Budgeting – Allocate every rupee to a purpose.

2. **Debt Management Tools**

   Government Loan Repayment & Consolidation Schemes

   ◈ RBI Loan Restructuring Scheme – Helps individuals manage loans.

   ◈ Mudra Loan (for Entrepreneurs) – Small business financing.

Debt Repayment Strategies

◊ Debt Snowball – Pay smallest loans first.

◊ Debt Avalanche – Pay high-interest loans first.

◊ Credit Card Balance Transfer – Reduce credit card interest using SBI, ICICI, HDFC, Axis balance transfer options.

Debt Tracking Apps

◊ Cred – Tracks and rewards credit card payments.

◊ Bajaj Finserv App – Manages loans and EMIs.

3. **Investment Platforms & Wealth-Building Tools.**

Stock Market Investing

◊ **Zerodha** – Low-cost stock and mutual fund investments.

◊ Groww—simplified stock, mutual fund, and gold investing.

◊ **Upstox** – Fast-growing brokerage with free Demat account.

Mutual Funds & SIPs

◊ **ET Money, Paytm Money** – Direct mutual fund investments.

◊ **Kuvera** – Zero-commission mutual fund investment platform.

◊ The AMFI (Association of Mutual Funds in India) provides research and insights on mutual funds.

Gold & Precious Metal Investments

◊ **Sovereign Gold Bonds (SGBs)** – Government-backed, interest-earning gold investment.

◊ **Digital Gold (Paytm, PhonePe, Google Pay)** – Small investment in gold.

Real Estate Investing

◊ **Fractional Ownership (Strata, hBits)** – Invest in high-value properties with small amounts.

◊ **REITs (Real Estate Investment Trusts)** – Invest in real estate like a stock (e.g., Embassy REIT, Mindspace REIT).

Alternative Investments

◊ **RBI Bonds** – Secure investment with stable returns.

◊ **Corporate FDs (Bajaj Finance, Mahindra Finance)** – Higher interest than bank FDs.

4. Income Diversification Tools

Multiple income sources accelerate financial freedom.

Freelancing & Gig Economy

◊ **WorknHire, Truelancer, FlexC** – Indian freelance job platforms.

◊ **Fiverr, Upwork** – Global freelance work

Content Creation & Digital Income

◊ **YouTube Partner Program** – Monetize video content.

◊ **Instagram Reels Bonus & Affiliate Marketing** – Earn from social media.

◊ **Amazon Associates, Flipkart Affiliate Program** – Earn from online sales commissions.

Online courses & e-learning

◊ **Unacademy, Udemy, Teachmint** – Sell courses and coaching.

Passive income sources

◊ **Dividend Stocks (HDFC, Infosys, Tata Steel)** – Earn from stock dividends.

◊ **Fixed Income Bonds (Bharat Bond ETF, PSU Bonds)** – Government-backed returns.

◊ **Rental Income & Co-Living Spaces (NestAway, NoBroker)** – Earn from property rental.

5. **Retirement Planning & Tax Optimization Tools**

Multiple streams of income speed up financial independence.

Side Hustle Platforms

Built On Freelancing — Upwork, Fiverr, Toptal.

Online courses and coaching – Teachable, Udemy, Coursera.

Affiliate Marketing – Amazon Associates, ShareASale

Stock Photography/Videos – Shutterstock, Adobe Stock

PASSIVE INCOME GENERATORS

Dividend Stocks – A third way of earning is through the dividend of the stocks.

Check out peer-to-peer lending — I used it on platforms that connect the non-profits to investors like Kiva and Prosper.

Dropshipping & E-commerce Automation – Meet Shopify, WooCommerce.

1. **Retirement tools and tax optimization tools**

Early retirement planning helps secure your financial future.

RETIREMENT ACCOUNTS & INVESTMENTS

Retirement Products: EPF & PPF (India), 401(k), IRA (USA)

NPS (National Pension Scheme in India) – Pension by the government.

Robo-advisors (Wealthfront, Betterment) — invest without hands.

2. **Personal Finance & Money-Mindset Tools**

The trouble is with money and the right mindset.

Books on Financial Freedom

Money and Mindset The Psychology of Money – Morgan Housel

Robert Kiyosaki: Rich Dad Poor Dad

MJ DeMarco – The Millionaire Fastlane

Podcasts & Blogs

Debt-free living – The Dave Ramsey Show

BiggerPockets – All things real estate investing.

Mr. Money Mustache — You don't have to be frugal to retire early.

Online Courses

Coursera, Udemy, Khan Academy: Personal finance courses

3. **Financial Protection & Emergency Funds**
   A safety net prevents financial setbacks.

Emergency Fund

3–6 months' worth of expenses in a high-yield savings account.

Insurance

Health Insurance – Covers medical emergencies.

Term Life Insurance – Protects family in case of loss of income. Disability insurance provides income protection against unforeseen events.

UNDERSTANDING FINANCIAL READINESS

College students and recent graduates, both in India and abroad, have found the journey toward financial independence to be quite challenging. Add to societal pressures and the complex realities surrounding debt and employment, and it becomes extremely important to have an objective look at financial habits. In this segment, we will go through a few more entertaining examples that you can apply to better yourself in terms of your financial literacy, the very basis of financial discipline.

Question #1: Are you ready to take control of your finances? The first step in gaining financial self-awareness is an honest assessment of your financial readiness. That's where specifically designed Financial Readiness Quiz can work wonders. This quiz aims to prompt you to consider closely how you spend and save your money. It asks simple questions to encourage the evaluator to reflect on things like budgeting habits, impulse buys, managing debt, and even basics like interest rates and investment principles. Knowing where you have gaps gives you a better understanding of where you stand financially and what you need to change to reach your goals.

Understanding your current level of financial literacy is crucial. Realizing what you don't know is the first step toward any improvement. We often plow through life without stopping to realize whether our financial decisions are informed choices or just habits. For example, developing a budget might be elementary, but for most of us, the larger aspirations — such as buying a home or retiring — are beyond our reach without it. Understanding financial topics at a deeper level can lead to making sound decisions and prepare you to participate in discussions surrounding money with more confidence.

Recognizing your strengths and weaknesses is another important element of attaining financial discipline. This self-reflection enables you to identify trends in habits, positive and negative. Are you a saver but have a hard time with discretionary spending? Or maybe you're great at budgeting but hesitant to buy? Identifying these attributes enables you to focus on refining strengths and remedying weaknesses. By formulating a focused action plan based on this assessment, you foster growth and synchronize your subsequent actions with your long-term objectives.

Understanding your financial literacy, however, is often a launchpad for more intentional actions. Understanding financial principles empowers you to set realistic goals and make informed choices. For instance, the idea that compound interest can supercharge both your savings or, if unchecked, your debt as well. Seeing it can also lead you to adopt more disciplined financial behaviors — such as making regular savings contributions or paying off debt more quickly. Understanding this can inspire a transition from reactive to proactive money management.

The next step entails providing guidelines for implementing the Financial Readiness Quiz to make it as effective as possible. Take this quiz with honesty and as much openness as possible so you can really face the truth of your financials. Schedule a distraction-free time for answering each question in this 3 — so you have ample context for your responses. Finally, after taking the quiz, review your results with a learning and growth mindset. Look for help with the more problematic areas you identify. Monitoring progress over time can help cement improvements and indicate areas where changes may be warranted.

The inclusion of these tools in your finances can greatly change your path toward financial independence. For young adults who are experiencing both the excitement and challenge of creating their own futures, the sense of empowerment that comes from greater financial literacy can be life-changing. The better a college student understands the long-term consequences of the financial decisions they are making, the more capable they will be able to resist societal pressures. Recent graduates can apply what they learned to approach debts and work opportunities more strategically.

None of that means that reaching financial discipline is an eventual or easy chore. It takes commitment, perseverance, and a desire to become a lifelong learner. But with the right tools and mind-set — and the tools discussed here — you have the power to turn uncertainty into confidence and complexity into clarity. Through assessment and optimization of your financial chains of habits, you are not only ensuring equilibrium; you are laying the foundation for long-term economic prosperity.

ANALYZING SPENDING HABITS

Smart Spending: How to Take Control of Your Finances

With our society constantly moving toward achieving financial independence, knowing how and when to spend can set the tone for the rest of your success. This is more true for young adults in India, college students at the beginning of their financial life, and graduate students after several rounds of job hunting. It is not merely useful but necessary to furnish tools to better analyze and manage spending behavior.

A daily spending review is the first step to controlling expenditure. This simple practice can bring attention to those sneaky, preventable costs we just have to be aware of. Things like making regular online purchases or going out to eat at restaurants on a regular basis may not feel like a big deal within a given week but can pile up quickly over weeks and months, cutting into your budget more than you expected. When you take the time each week or month to look where your money goes, you'll probably find places you can cut back." Think of it a little like having a financial health check-up — you can't know how "sick" or well you are if you don't ever get checked.

This awareness of your spending habits enables you to adjust your budget more deliberately. This awareness serves as your personal finance compass, guiding you through your unique financial landscape. For instance, if you have an ongoing expense for all the entertainment subscriptions that you rarely use, you may want to channel that money into your savings or pay off a high-interest debt. Crucially, it doesn't mean making radical lifestyle changes — just making better choices based on what you have. The adjustments you make — and the little choices you make — can add up, potentially creating healthy savings and a more equitable distribution of your money.

A clear picture of your expenses, in turn, helps you in developing and prioritizing your financial goals. Tracking every rupee lets someone choose what is most important to them financially. Whether that's saving for a home purchase, planning a vacation, or building an emergency fund, having a deeply analytical view of your spending routine gives you ownership of these aspirations. For example, if you're in the life stage where you have dreamt of travelling abroad, knowing your expenditure enables you to create a travel-saving plan and make that goal a reality, instead of just a dream. High-definition budgets sharpen their focus and allow for granular decisions that closely map to near-term wants and long-term dreams.

Overspending involves spending money, not just earning and managing your money. Young adults, particularly college students and recent grads, have a tough time tracking their spending. The reality? Those little, seemingly negligible costs accumulate. Over time, these seemingly insignificant expenses, such as daily coffee, late-night food deliveries, and streaming subscriptions, can significantly reduce your budget without your knowledge.

But the good news? You don't need to make extreme sacrifices in your lifestyle to develop smart financial habits. The trick is to uncover how you spend and make intentional choices in line with your priorities.

STEP 1: SPOT THE LEAKS IN YOUR SPENDING

Ever checked your bank statement and wondered where all your money went? You're not alone.

Start by tracking your spending for a month. Every rupee. Every purchase. Whether it's an app subscription or a dinner outing, note it down. While it may seem tedious, examining your spending habits in detail can be enlightening.

- Are you spending more on takeout than groceries?
- Do you have multiple subscriptions you barely use?
- Are impulse purchases eating into your savings?

Awareness is the first step toward financial control. You don't have to make drastic changes, just small, mindful adjustments that help you prioritize.

STEP 2: CATEGORIZE & CUT DOWN WISELY

Once you know where your money is going, break your expenses into essential and non-essential categories.

- Essentials: rent, utilities, groceries, transportation, medical bills.

- Non-Essentials: Streaming services, eating out, online shopping, entertainment.

This doesn't mean you must cut out all non-essentials—but it helps you decide what's worth keeping and what's just draining your wallet.

For example:

If you're paying for four different streaming services, do you really need all of them?

Love dining out? Try limiting it to weekends or special occasions.

Spending on random online shopping? Give yourself a 24-hour rule before making a purchase.

By making small, intentional tweaks, you create space for more savings without sacrificing enjoyment.

STEP 3: SET GOALS THAT ACTUALLY STICK

Saying "I need to save more money" is vague. Instead, set a clear, specific goal that keeps you motivated.

- Bad Goal: "I should start saving soon."

- Good Goal: "I will save ₹5,000 per month for six months for my emergency fund."

Having a number, a timeline, and a purpose makes it easier to follow through. Want to travel? Save up for it. Planning to buy a new phone? Create a savings plan instead of swiping your credit card.

A small but steady savings habit adds up overtime.

STEP 4: TRACK PROGRESS & ADJUST WHEN NEEDED

Life is unpredictable. Some months, you might exceed your savings goal. Other months, unexpected expenses might set you back. That's okay!

The key is to check in regularly and adjust when needed. Simple ways to track progress:

- Use an Expense Tracker – Apps like Walnut, Money View, or even a simple Excel sheet.

- Review your budget, spending, and savings each month to determine whether any adjustments are necessary.

- Celebrate Small Wins – Each milestone (₹10K saved, loan paid off) is progress toward financial freedom!

Being flexible keeps you in control without feeling restricted.

FINAL THOUGHT: FINANCIAL FREEDOM STARTS WITH AWARENESS

Most financial stress doesn't come from not making enough money, it comes from not knowing where it's going.

- Track your spending.
- Identify what matters most.
- Set realistic goals.
- Check your progress & adjust.

Small changes today can completely transform your financial future. The more intentional you are with your money, the more freedom you create for yourself.

EVALUATING DEBT STATUS

A Young Adult's Plan to Take Control of Their Debt

For many young adults in India — particularly college students and recent graduates — debt can be a heavy weight. It may be student loans, credit card bills, or personal loans, and it's simple to feel overwhelmed. However, the secret solution to financial freedom isn't necessarily earning more—it's learning how to manage and strategically eliminate debt.

Let's put it in simple steps that you can take and make actionable.

STEP 1: KNOW EXACTLY HOW MUCH YOU OWE

It sounds obvious, but people are often afraid to face their total debt. No point in pretending it's not there! Write down every loan, credit card balance, and outstanding payment.

- ◆ Write down:

  The total amount you owe

  The rate of interest for each liability

  The required minimum monthly payment

  This straightforward exercise provides you with a comprehensive understanding. It's like having directions — without it, you're just guessing where to go."

STEP 2: IDENTIFY HIGH-INTEREST DEBTS (AND CRUSH THEM FIRST)

There are good debts and bad debts. Some, including credit cards and payday loans, accrue interest quickly; these are the ones you want to target first.

- ◆ The Avalanche Method: A system that helps you pay off the debt with the highest interest first while still making the minimum payments on the other debts. This is the most savings over the long term.

- The Snowball Method: If you struggle to stay motivated, pick the smallest debt and pay it off quickly. The feeling of unencumbering yourself builds momentum to slay bigger ones.

Example: Let's say you have:

- A ₹50,000 credit card debt at 18% interest

- Personal loan, ₹1,00,000; 7% interest

Which one should you pay down first? The credit card! You will pay more overtime with the higher interest, even if the balance is lower.

STEP 3: TRACK YOUR PROGRESS & STAY MOTIVATED

Have you ever tried to lose weight without tracking what you eat? The same applies to managing debt — logging progress that keeps you accountable.

- Use a budgeting app such as Walnut or Money View to track payments.

- Reminder due dates and avoid being behind in your bills.

- Use a visual tracker (like a chart, a checklist, a whiteboard, etc.) to celebrate small wins.

  Real World Application: A recent grad swimming in debt decided to hang a "debt thermometer" on their wall. Every time they did ₹5,000 — they colored an area with a marker. Tracking their progress was really what helped them stay motivated!

STEP 4: AVOID COMMON DEBT TRAPS

Young professionals often take out loans to repay older ones. This results in perpetual debt. Here's how to avoid it:

- Do not simply pay the minimum balance — this keeps you in debt longer.

- Don't consider new loans while paying old loans — It's alluring but adds more to financial pressure.

- Watch out for "Buy Now, Pay Later" schemes — They are easy, but you can really accumulate with them quickly.

Instead, pay more toward your EMI as and when you can. Even ₹2,000 more per month can save you thousands as interest in the long run!

STEP 5: VISUALIZE YOUR DEBT-FREE FUTURE

And it's not just about the numbers — it's about peace of mind. Imagine:

- No anxiety about due dates.

- Extra savings for travel, investment, or a home

- Confidence that you can manage your money

Debt freedom doesn't mean you have to make massive sacrifices — it means you need to be deliberate. Every little action you take today makes you one step closer to financial independence.

Start now. One smart decision at a time.

TRACKING FINANCIAL PROGRESS

Monitoring your financial activity through financial methods is a crucial aspect of achieving financial freedom, akin to using a map to navigate unfamiliar territory. It helps identify the so-called "spending leaks," or those areas where money is potentially seeping out each month without you even realizing it. These are monthly expenses leaks that seem insignificant but add up over time. Tracking your total spending is a reputable way of keeping an eye on your own habits! Knowing this empowers you to make smarter cuts that enable you to spend less, save more, and make wise decisions.

The Monthly Expense Tracker is one useful tool for that. By using it regularly, you're able to break down your spending into needs, such as rent and food shopping, and wants, such as eating out or that third latte of your morning commute. This categorization enables you to easily see where you can cut and which areas. If you find that dining out makes up a large percentage of your budget, you can adjust, like meal prep at home. It's about finding the right mix that works with your broader financial objectives.

Following up on what you pay is also important. By diligently tracking these bills and loan payments, you not only avoid paying late fees, but you also worry less about going into debt. With a packed schedule, keeping up with due dates can be challenging, but reminders or a Debt Repayment Tracker can promote consistency. Debt can be intimidating, and many young graduates just starting out in the adult world are facing student debt alongside new living expenses. This also allows you to break down the debt repayments into bite-sized, achievable targets, which will keep you motivated. Every repaid debt is a little win that rewards positive behavior and instills confidence in your money management skills.

By regularly reflecting on your goals, making sure that they still fit in with your current life is a valuable exercise. Life is constantly changing — new jobs, moving to a new city, or starting a family. All of these can affect your financial plans. Taking a few hours each month or quarter to remember what you were working toward and what was important will allow you to make sure that your financial strategies have not become misaligned with your aspirations. This way, you will not be bound to outdated goals, and your financial plan will be fluid and adaptable.

Using a goal achievement checklist can help you with this. This checklist serves as a physical reminder of your big-picture goals and smaller, incremental steps you can take along the way. Reviewing this checklist regularly helps you celebrate achievements, however minor. Whether you're achieving a savings milestone or successfully paying off a credit card bill, it's important to celebrate these achievements. Recognizing These Wins Creates a Positive Reinforcing Feedback Loop Celebrating this achievement gives a feeling of victory and acts as a motivational agent — telling our system that, yes, we can do this — let us take further actions.'

When young adults, such as college students setting out on their financial journeys, are bombarded with societal pressures to spend, it can be difficult to make the right decision. While there is nothing wrong with enjoying a certain lifestyle, there is a temptation to overspend, and that is part of why it can be difficult to remain disciplined. Yet, when you add the monitoring of various financial activities to your daily practice, you shield yourself from these external factors. It's crucial to maintain focus on the goal, rather than succumbing to fleeting desires influenced by social pressure.

Recent graduates, however, must navigate a competitive job market while unloading debts, often hangers-on from their freshly minted degrees. This is where the exercise of reviewing financial aspirations is even more important. With careers and income streams in flux, impairment in adopting financial plans can make a vital difference for a smoother transition to stable financial health.

FINAL INSIGHTS

In this chapter, we have discussed the key interactive tools and practices that encourage financial discipline, especially among young adults in India, college students, and recent graduates. We examined the reasons behind financial readiness and why honest self-assessments are crucial and walked through tools such as the Financial Readiness Quiz. Assessing your financial literacy is an important first step that can help you figure out your personal strengths and weaknesses and point the way to better habits. We stressed that understanding financial concepts such as budgeting, managing debt, and investment fundamentals empowers you. This foundation fosters proactive engagement and supports readers in pushing back against societal pressures and making responsible choices around money.

In addition, we discussed techniques such as monitoring spending behavior and classifying outlays to gain insights into financial habits. Identifying opportunities for budgeting adjustments supports realistic target setting for a household. By using bookmarkers for reflection and indicators for steps made over time, the payer can adjust the financial plans continuously to flow with the dynamics of their lives. Finding financial freedom takes time and effort, but it can be life-changing as it converts fear and uncertainty into faith and certainty. By embedding this knowledge and these tools into their daily practices, young people and new graduates alike can confidently steer their financial futures toward sustainable economic well-being.

Chapter 11

CONCLUSION

CHANGING FINANCIAL HABITS

We conduct data collection on the ground until October 2023. Income and spending within the nation have seen undiscovered trends and patterns, which this chapter explores through the preparatory mediums of culture and technology. These changes are altering the ways that young adults navigate their finances, affecting their decisions about borrowing and spending. Consumer behavior is evolving, as we noted, with an increasing willingness to take on debt for aspirational spending. This marks a shift away from conventional perspectives on loans, raising curiosity about what's changed and what it means for how we manage our finances.

From a narrative perspective, the chapter depicts the complexities that underlie the fortunes of India's economic development. It speaks to how the trends of rising digital payments, consumer borrowing, and credit card usage are linked to societal expectations for young professionals and job seekers, influencing personal finance strategies among students and those fresh out of university. The text will educate readers on the concept of smart borrowing and how to distinguish between needs and lifestyle desires. Furthermore, the text emphasizes the significance of financial literacy and education as essential weapons in addressing a series of modern-day monetary obstacles. This chapter offers a comprehensive guide to navigating the complexities of financial independence as they relate to technology, culture, and more in an ever-evolving landscape.

EVOLVING FINANCIAL BEHAVIOR

Demography of Finance: How You Are Spending and Borrowing Differently

The financial fabric of India is changing — and fast. No longer is borrowing reserved for life's biggest expenditures — purchasing a home, financing an education, or launching a business. Lending today extends, however, beyond the need. They are about lifestyle, aspirations, and convenience.

Young professionals are redefining the concept of 'debt' as we know it, whether it's paying off the newest iPhone or borrowing personal loans for extravagant holidays. What was once deemed risky or even taboo is quickly becoming a financial norm. The new confidence in borrowing can be a good thing, but with this comfort comes a need for awareness, responsibility, and balance.

Going from Saving to Spending: A Generational Mindset Shift

For past generations, financial discipline was saved first, spend later. If you wanted something, you waited until you had enough cash in hand. Today? It's instant gratification in a salted-butter shell.

Young adults are using credit to pay for lifestyle upgrades with growing comfort — be it a high-end gadget, a designer change of clothing or an exotic holiday. It's not just a matter of spending more but spending differently. Loans aren't just for needs anymore — they're for wants.

It was a change that financial institutions were swift to acknowledge. Now banks and fintech companies have personal loans and easy EMI options catering to this kind of spending behavior. No paperwork. There are no extended waiting periods. Talk about a few clicks on a smartphone and boom — credit approved. It's smooth, speedy, and — at times — perilously enticing.

The Danger of Impulsive Borrowing

When credit is so freely available, it's simple to overspend. Many youngsters, swayed by their EMI dreams, overlook the long-term effect of their financial habits.

₹3,000 as an EMI for a new phone doesn't sound like much. Factor in another ₹5,000 for a vacation loan. More ₹2,500 for premium gym membership. Pretty soon, these little monthly obligations balloon into a cash drain that siphons savings and constricts future possibilities.

It's easy to succumb to the cycle of taking on debt now and worrying later.

But bad debt can bring housing:

- Reduced savings — leaving you no safety net for emergencies.

- Increase in interest payments — reducing future income.

- A tarnished credit score — which will make loans in the future (home or car loans, for example) more difficult to get.

The key? Borrow smart. It's not just about borrowing because you can, but it also makes financial sense.

Advent of Cashless Transactions

Another major transformation is underway beyond borrowing — the transition from cash to digital payments.

Until recently, cash held a dominant position in India's economy. But with UPI, mobile wallets, and contactless payments, young Indians are entering the digital finance space more than ever.

Why? Because it's quick, easy and sometimes rewarding.

- Cashbacks & Discounts – Digital wallets provide incentives that make the transaction more appealing.

- Expense Tracking – The apps aid in monitoring the spending habits of users in real-time.

- Security – Online payments are now safer and more dependable, thanks to high-end encryption.

Digital payments seem to be an ideal fit in the fast-paced, tech-driven world of college students and young professionals. The shift to cashless transactions is not just about convenience — it's about efficiency, control, and access.

And even in rural areas, where banks have long been scarce, digital platforms have brought most people into the financial system. This shift isn't only altering spending habits — it's democratizing access to finances.

What This Means for the Future

India's financial behavior is undergoing a turbocharged transformation. A new economy is taking shape, driven by aspirational spending and digital transactions. But these changes bring with them responsibility and awareness.

- Borrow wisely. Credit is a tool, not a temptation: Use it strategically, not impulsively.

- Track your spending. These small EMIs quickly add up, and you do not realize it.

- Embrace digital finance. But watch out for hidden fees and impulse buys.

That is the future of money in India: It's not how much you have; it's how smart you are about managing it.

SOCIETY EXPECTATIONS AND FINANCIAL DISCIPLINE

If you're someone who likes to keep up with what society wants you to do, maybe that's why so many people spend more than they have — they're trying to keep up with whatever they think their peers are doing. In India especially this pressure can be high as one's social standing can sometimes be directly tied to their belongings and manifesting their wealth in a way. These pressures can be influential among young adults aged 18 to 29 years, including college students and recent graduates, and threaten financial stability.

And it all begins with the group to which we belong. You should be in the right shape and size to demonstrate all that your physical belongings, gadgets, automobiles, suits, and expensive diet business can accomplish in public. And that impulse toward consistency contributes to behaviors — like overconsumption — that can threaten personal finances. Keeping up with our peers and coworkers can lead to stress, more debt, and a diversion from your personal financial goals.

Social media compounds these pressures by enabling relentless peer comparison. It creates a context in which individuals tend to represent only the high points of their experience, where luxury and accomplishment rule. For those in their early career who use the trendy TR as a single reflection of their life, it may resemble a success ledger. The constant secondhand exposure to aspirational lifestyles from influencers and peers on (or in) Instagram and Facebook can make feelings of inadequacy or missing out feel more raw." Young adults may purchase things or experiences they can flaunt as validation of their achievements while falling into their own cycles of excess spending to obtain them.

Still, resisting these pressures takes education and awareness. Also, one practical approach could be increasing awareness about the difference between needs and wants. You have made progress in the current year. The first thing to do is analyze your spending. Determine whether the purchase is necessary or merely a result of your fleeting societal greed. The eye-opening activity where you put all your expenses into a 'needs' vs. 'wants' list can clarify where exactly your money goes.

Being mindful about the financial decisions one makes is a great way to combat some of the effects of societal pressure. Mindfulness moves you from instant gratification to long-term financial health. Financial independence and stability bring more joy than a few new items ever will. Setting your own personal financial goals is also key to staying grounded. Armed with the knowledge that the goals we decide to pursue are based on our values, rather than society's, financial decisions will be far easier to work out.

A candid, transparent discussion around finances is the best way to create a supportive environment. Rather than viewing conversations about finances as taboo, discussing Bill with friends, family members, or mentors can provide new viewpoints and alleviate some of the social pressures. These discussions can change the narrative around differing financial paths and develop a responsible spending message more reflective of parents' present reality.

Practicing delayed gratification can also help curb socially induced impulse purchasing. Rather than acting on an impulse, wait a designated period — 30 days, for example — before purchasing an item to see if the desire to buy remains when the impulse to buy has receded. Time often eliminates the impulse, saving you money and avoiding regret.

That is why you need to educate yourself about finance. Building financial literacy for young adults, students, and freshmen is a beneficial step forward to help them cope with this pressure. Knowing how to budget, save, and invest wisely is a useful foundation for better decision-making potential. Raising awareness about managing societal pressures can serve as a foundation for implementing education-oriented meetings on financial health.

For optimal financial health, sometimes we must say no to budget-busting social invites or purchases. It's impolite to beg for a peer to accompany us on our rounds. Respect is essential in the classroom as opposed to on the job. True friends will understand these choices and may even appreciate the candidness, prompting a group investigation of socializing and spending like never before.

CULTURAL INFLUENCES ON SPENDING

India, a country renowned for its diversity and rich cultural heritage, closely links its financial habits to cultural values and social behaviors. The realities of the consequences of the metals industry, social structure, and politics all mingle and intertwine with their daily lives, imbuing how citizens approach money and saving. An understanding of these cultural impacts is essential for young adults on their financial journeys.

A big way culture influences financial habits is through the stories it tells that conflate ownership and status. Many Indian communities view property ownership, or the possession of luxury goods, as a sign of success. It is this absolute wish to indulge that tends to prioritize instant gratification rather than sustainable economic strategies.

For instance, there could be significant pressure to purchase a house or car early in one's career, even if it means depleting one's finances. This inclination may lead to cumbersome loans and a lack of savings, both of which could provide a safety net and future possibilities.

For example, think about the culture behind weddings. Weddings are also the most important of Indian festivals and a representation of prosperity and family reputation. Families might lavishly spend on weddings, sometimes to the point of going into debt, the belief being that these celebrations symbolize social class. Although this spending fosters happiness and strengthens ties within a community, it can also leave people with a crunch in financial management after the celebration. Weighing the short-term thrill of a big event against its long-term financial viability is crucial.

Cultural expectations also heavily dictate spending habits in festivals and cultural events. Diwali, Eid, or Christmas celebrations are occasions of joy for the whole nation but can put a strain on personal budgets because of the expenses related to gifts, decor, and festivities. While these moments strengthen community bonds, they also exacerbate financial strains. For those who have recently entered the workforce or are still in school, the cumulative impact of annual festival expenses can significantly deplete their savings, which could be better allocated towards life-changing investments such as education or emergencies.

Such a cultural tendency to spend during the festival season calls for prudent budgeting, however. Planning and allotting specific amounts for festive seasons ensures individuals enjoy celebrations without hindering their financial well-being. Choosing meaningful — but affordable — ways to celebrate can help uphold cultural rituals without potentially jeopardizing one's finances.

Family dynamics channel financial priorities through women, balancing contradictory expectations around personal finances that can undermine financial autonomy. In many families, there is a family-wide focus of support for older members or younger siblings, which reconfigures individual financial goals. Family needs can often take precedence over ambitions, whether it is saving for your own college education or self-improvement. This is especially true in joint family systems where cooperation in money management for the collective good is common but comes with a set of challenges.

Maria Santos, 29, reflecting on the wheels of familial responsibility, added, "We do this because we hear that this is what we have to do, but in terms of family, out culture at the bottom line is: You go home, you show up, we take care of you, so is this why we don't say anything?"

To help mitigate the risks of financial failure, opening communication about financial goals within families can help reach a better mutual understanding of how to allocate resources. Doing so can spur conversations about both personal and collective financial goals that can lead to finding a more harmonious way forward for planning that keeps cultural traditions intact through new marital unions while allowing room for personal development.

I remember you also had a financial independence goal, and it is beneficial that, in a time when more people want to achieve financial independence, you have figured out what you want personally, without letting the family pressure you. Young professionals and students — learning to establish clear boundaries and communicate personal financial goals is essential. Having savings accounts for individual milestones and managing shared family responsibilities alongside them promotes an individual's autonomy and accomplishes long-lasting financial independence.

The influence of culture on financial habits is quintessential, especially as India intertwines its diverse cultural heritage with modernity. Understanding the line between maintaining family values and becoming financially independent enables young adults to find their own trajectories. To know more: Indulgence: How to live a rich cultural life without breaking the bank?

PRACTICAL FINANCIAL STRATEGIES

The foundation of any wellness goes back to the budget. For young adults in India who are likely just starting their careers or pursuing higher education, the first step to mastering personal finance is monitoring their income and expenses. A comprehensive budget sheds light on spending patterns that distinguish between essential and discretionary spending. They will be the call to action to help people understand where their money ends up every month and where they can save unnecessary money.

For instance, consider Riya, a recent graduate who is about to start her first job in Bangalore. She soon discovered that it was impossible to track her spending without a budget. Riya figured out where she could save by writing down her monthly income, as well as regular expenses like rent, groceries, and transportation. Not only did this practice help her cut costs, but it also meant she'd be able to put more toward her top priorities, like saving an emergency fund.

When you build a budget, it's important to factor in room for the unforeseen.

However, life can be unpredictable, resulting in unexpected expenses such as medical emergencies or urgent repairs. It is therefore prudent to keep aside a fraction of the monthly earnings as a cushion. This part of budgeting gives peace.

This aspect of budgeting ensures financial stability by preparing for unforeseen events. Introducing regular savings later on is crucial for one's financial future. Having a regular savings plan is like an insurance policy, protecting you against surprising expenses and accumulating reserves for later projects or purchases. One solution is to treat savings like an expense you must pay — rather than one you want to pay. For example, if you have automatic transfers from checking to a savings account shortly after you get your paycheck, you will save in a disciplined manner.

Don't underestimate the power of compound interest. Even relatively small, regular deposits in a savings account can add up overtime. Consider an individual, Aman — a collegegoer who decided to save Rs. 500 every month. His savings grew considerably, even beyond what he thought it would be, due to interest accumulation over the next several years. This underscores the need to start early and persist in pursuing any savings goals.

Additionally, a regular deposit plan can help secure you in difficult times like recession or job loss. Its cushion reduces the tensions inherent in the state of financial insecurity. This sense of security allows individuals to focus on long-term goals, such as pursuing further education, establishing a new business, or embarking on travels.

The other major factor in financial health is debt management. Debt adds up fast in our consumer culture, particularly for young adults trying to live up to their social circles and comparable lifestyles. This may require prioritizing the payoff of high-interest debt, such as credit card debt, to prevent it from spiraling out of control if left unpaid. These debts are prioritized first because they relieve the financial burden of debt overall and save money — because even a few extra years of paying down an interest-only debt comes at an expensive cost.

Students and recent graduates need to know what taking on student loans means, too. No one should rely on loans, so they should be careful to keep on top of repayments and look for opportunities to consolidate or refinance loans to reduce the overall cost. This made me realize how taking proactive measures to tackle these debts not only helps with credit scores but also paves the path to financial freedom.

For example, consider Arun, who was overwhelmed with multiple debts (e.g., student loans, credit card) "Yes, you need to have a game plan to pay off debt, but one that is focused on the higher interest rates," he says, adding that he was able to pay off smaller debts first in order to build momentum and motivation for larger debts. In turn, he took back control of his finances and felt less financial stress.

These practices — budgeting, saving, and managing debt — are all discipline and patience. For the most part, though, when you do them consistently, they yield sustainable financial well-being. As aspiring young adults take their steps on this journey towards financial independence, adopting these actionable, tech-aided strategies will ensure their emergence through present-day challenges and thrive towards economic freedom in India's diverse landscape in the years to come.

Stepping toward financial well-being can be intimidating, but breaking it down into manageable steps can help. A budget brings clarity and control; savings (of whatever amount) bring resilience and security; and managing debt well frees you from its shackles. These are all critical components of a comprehensive strategy for controlling personal finances and ensuring a stable future.

THE ROLE OF FINANCIAL EDUCATION

Why Financial Literacy Matters for Young Adults Managing money isn't just about making more of it, it's about knowing how to use it wisely. For young adults, especially college students and recent graduates, financial literacy is the key to staying ahead of debt, making smart investments, and avoiding common financial traps. t's about understanding money and how to use it, not just budgeting.

THE FIRST STEP: KNOWING WHAT YOU'RE GETTING INTO

Consider this: as you transition into adulthood, you encounter significant financial choices.

The list of financial options is endless, including student loans, credit cards, savings plans, and investments. Without the right knowledge, these decisions can either set you up for success or trap you in years of financial stress.

Take student loans, for example. Many students sign up for them without fully understanding the interest rates, repayment terms, or the long-term cost of borrowing. A financially literate person, however, would know how to compare loan options, calculate repayment strategies, and even find ways to pay off their debt faster. The difference? Financial literacy turns financial survival into financial stability.

Dodging Financial Traps

It's easy to fall for predatory lending if you don't know what to look for. "No credit check loans!" "Easy instant approval!" Sounds tempting, right? But behind these offers are often sky-high interest rates and hidden fees designed to keep borrowers in a cycle of debt.

A financially aware individual can spot the red flags—such as unreasonable interest rates, misleading repayment terms, or vague contract details. Simply put, knowledge is power. The more you know about how financial systems operate, the harder it becomes for lenders to take advantage of you.

Demystifying Financial Jargon

For a lot of young adults, terms like APR, compound interest, asset allocation, or mutual funds might as well be in another language. And because these concepts sound intimidating, many people choose to ignore them altogether. But that's a mistake—because once you break them down, you realize they're not as complicated as they seem.

For instance, let's say you get your first credit card. You see a "0% introductory APR for 12 months" offer and assume it's a great deal. But what happens after 12 months? A financially literate person would know how to check for high post-introductory interest rates, hidden fees, or penalties for late payments. They'd also know how to use a credit card wisely, paying the full balance on time, keeping their credit utilization low, and avoiding unnecessary debt.

With the right financial knowledge, you stop fearing financial terms and start using them to your advantage.

Breaking Financial Myths

There are a lot of misconceptions about money floating around. Some people think investing is only for the rich. Others believe they don't need to start saving until they're making a big salary. Both beliefs are false.

Investing isn't gambling. The stock market has risks, but with the right strategies, it can be a powerful tool for growing wealth over time. Even small, consistent investments can lead to significant gains in the long run.

Saving isn't just for the wealthy. It's about discipline, not income level. Even setting aside ₹500 a month can build a solid financial cushion over time. The earlier you start, the better. One of the most important financial concepts to learn is the time value of money—basically, money today is worth more than the same amount in the future because it has the potential to grow when invested. Understanding this encourages young professionals to start saving and investing early, whether for retirement, an emergency fund, or future goals.

BUILDING A STRONG FINANCIAL FOUNDATION

Financial literacy isn't just about making more money, it's about being in control of your financial future. Whether it's understanding loans, avoiding scams, learning investment basics, or simply budgeting smarter, having the right knowledge can change your entire financial trajectory.

And here's the good news: You don't need a degree in finance to make smart financial choices. There are countless free online courses, financial tools, and budgeting apps that can help you get started. The key is to stay curious, keep learning, and apply what you learn.

At the end of the day, financial literacy is more than just knowing how to balance a budget—it's about making sure your money is working for you, not against you.

SUMMARY AND REFLECTIONS

Finances — Understand and adapt to changing financial habits of Indian young adults, particularly college students and recent graduates. This chapter explored how a concern with aspirational spending made possible by personal loans and credit yields a new moral order around debt. The trend has permeated the lives of young professionals, as loans have transformed into lifestyle objectives, now perceived as opportunities rather than a perpetual burden. But it is important for people to make smart financial decisions to avoid the strain of mishandled debt in the long run. Digital payment schemes are transforming the payment space, offering ease and convenience of access while also contributing to financial inclusion—particularly among tech-savvy youth. The development of these regular habits shows the importance of literacy and awareness in creating a healthy relationship with your finances.

Due to social pressure, norms and culture, materialistic desires and comparisons with others on social media, young adults experience the need to achieve everything simultaneously. "Awareness of these drivers and some prudent budgeting will help protect financial health." Teaching young people, the difference between needs and wants is a way to help them manage spending, establish personal financial goals, and reinforce positive money behaviors that align with their personal values. This is where financial literacy proves invaluable, empowering individuals to make sound decisions pertaining to loans and investments. Nurturing discussions around finances and encouraging mindfulness can help build immunity to an external environment and prepare for a more independent future with greater economic security as the markets and economy undergo change.

www.ingramcontent.com/pod-product-compliance
Lightning Source LLC
Chambersburg PA
CBHW020322180726
47991CB00018B/344